I Classici del

20 Great Italian Games

Games

By Giancarlo Rinaldi

Giancarlo Rinaldi was the founder and editor of the UK's best-known Italian football fanzine of the early 1990s, Rigore!. He also co-authored a guide to Serie A with Ray Della Pietra and wrote the local history books From the Serchio to the Solway and Great Dumfries Stories. A regular contributor to Football Italia magazine and now Soccer Italia and Soccer 360, he lives in Dumfries with his wife, Anne, and two children, Mia and Luca. A long-suffering Fiorentina fan, he has seen their holy Trinity of Giancarlo Antognoni, Roberto Baggio and Gabriel Batistuta in action and hopes to live to see their third Scudetto. You can follow him on that Twitter thing as @ginkers.

To Luca – The boy who helped me fall back in love with football.

Contents

Foreword

When I helped bring Italian football to the British screens back in 1992, I didn't realise what a watershed moment that would become. Who wants to watch boring catenaccio? That was the common response from the newspapers when Chrysalis Sport, via Channel 4, first announced the deal. But what was there to lose? With Sky's sporting empire restricted to one live match on Sunday afternoons and terrestrial television showing only recorded highlights, there was a hole in the schedule. With Serie A's full programme of matches all kicking off at 2pm – 1pm British time – that gap could be filled.

Not just by any sporting pap. But by games featuring the very top players in the world. With the English Premier League currently holding the purse strings and Spain's La Liga attracting world stars like Lionel Messi and Cristiano Ronaldo, some may forget that Italy was **THE** place to be in the early and mid-90s working under such coaches as Arrigo Sacchi, Fabio Capello, Marcello Lippi, Claudio Ranieri, Dino Zoff and Sven Goran Eriksson.

From Aldair to Zola, they were all there. Italian giants like Franco Baresi, Paolo Maldini, Gianluca Vialli, Roberto Mancini, Roby Baggio, Beppe Signori and World Cup hero Toto Schillaci. Dutch superstars Marco Van Basten, Frank Rijkaard and Ruud Gullit. Colombian Tino Asprilla. Denmark's Brian Laudrup who followed brother Michael to the peninsula. There was Brazil's Claudio Taffarel and Julio Cesar. Germany's Jurgen Kohler and Andreas Moller. Argentinians Claudio Caniggia and Gabriel Batistuta. The superstars' list just goes on and on.

Of course, we had an extra bonus. Gazza. The mercurial Paul Gascoigne had signed up to spend three years in Rome and was our launching pad. Even though there were other British stars plying their trade in Serie A just before and just afterwards like David Platt, Des Walker and Paul Ince, Gazza lit the touch-paper for us. Inevitably and despite the hype, he wasn't fit enough to play in our opening match. But we went ahead covering his team, Lazio, against Sampdoria. As the critics predicted, it was a boring draw. Only 3-3. But things perked up the next week as we watched Milan pip Pescara 5-4. In week five we had the Rossoneri beating Fiorentina 7-3.

Having installed the unknown James Richardson into the hot-seat and got a cult following for the Gazzetta Football Italia show he fronted on Saturday mornings, the response to the matches and our productions was amazing. Just one complaint. How can we learn more about all the teams and all the players in Serie A?

"What about producing a magazine to accompany the show?" asked Chrysalis sports supremo Neil Duncanson. Strange to think now that this was pre-website days. Why not? I could fit it in between editing both weekly Channel 4 shows…

But what I needed was some input from knowledgeable journalists on Italian football who were good writers in English, could be relied upon to hit deadlines and who were enthusiastic about the whole idea. Enter Giancarlo Rinaldi.

It's taken me a long while to get down to the reason for writing this note, but my introduction to Italian football only came about by becoming involved in those early television days. Giancarlo was inducted at birth. That passion evolved through his Italian ancestry and shaped his writing. If our fiery stats man Ray Della Pietra didn't know something, Giancarlo did. He was never stumped. His love of the Italian game shone through – especially if he was penning articles on his beloved Fiorentina.

But I quickly learned that GR was the man to go to if I also wanted knowledgeable articles on Italian football topics other than the Viola. Over 20 years later that penetrating insight is still valued by my team and I as the Football Italia website, to which Giancarlo regularly contributes, has outlasted the original magazine and the much-missed Italia programmes of Channel 4.

You may not agree with all 20 choices of his that follow. But you can be assured they are games that touched his heart. Sit back and enjoy – just like I have with the author's writings of the past two decades. Long may they continue. *Forza Italia. Forza Rinaldi.*

John D Taylor 2013
www.football-italia.net

Introduction

When I discuss football nowadays, I often feel quite old. As the talk turns to the best player ever seen or worst team witnessed, I can't help but think a lot of people are looking through a narrow window. At most their mind will stretch back five or six years, mine starts flitting back through the decades.

It is not as if I am actually that old. My first time-stamped football memory is of defending Italy to my Holland-supporting primary four teacher during the 1978 World Cup. I can only really remember games from that date onwards and, even then, with varying degrees of accuracy. However, in these days of social media and 24 hour news, 30-odd years of memories feel like an aeon.

I have always been fascinated by the history of the game before those matches I actually witnessed with my own eyes. I grew up on stories of Sandro Mazzola, Gianni Rivera and Gigi Riva and great nights of Italian sides battling with their Scottish or English counterparts in epic encounters. I was hooked by those tales of a time which helped to cement a vision of Serie A as negative, cynical and defensive among UK residents for decades to come.

As I started to delve into the archives, I found my imagination fired by the whole meandering plot of Italian football from its origins to the present day. From the English ex-pats who set up many club sides to Vittorio Pozzo's double World Cup winners; from the five-in-a-row Juventus team of the 1930s to the Grande Torino lost in the Superga disaster; from Gigi Meroni to Renato Curi; from *Totonero* to *Calciopoli* – it was a story of drama, achievement, tragedy, scandal and style which I found irresistible.

It also helped to fuel my contrary nature. There is nothing better than when people are arguing over which modern day star is the finest to ever grace the game than to throw in the name of somebody who has been dead for 50 years. That really adds another element to the debate.

And so I started writing down my memories of some of the best games I had ever seen and also tried to capture the essence of some great encounters I wish I had been around to witness. Looking back on the fixtures gives, I think, a context to their present-day equivalents. The clash of the colours of the clubs involved has echoes through history. I find it almost impossible to watch a live game without thinking of some previous encounter from several seasons ago.

This collection is a kind of edited highlights package of works which have been published on a number of websites and also my own blog. I have tried to pick out something that should appeal to fans of most of the top teams in Italy. Although I do realise that Fiorentina may be over-represented in the collection – but I make no apology for that. It's my ball, as we used to say in the school playground.

But I hope there is something for everyone in these pages. They are, understandably, focussed on the Golden Age of the Italian game which I was lucky enough to live through in the late 1980s and early 1990s when Serie A teams reigned supreme. However, they sweep through most other *Calcio* eras too.

For those who saw the games in question, I hope their retelling helps to rekindle some of the emotions felt at the time. For those too young or too distant to have seen the action, my aim is to give a crash-course in what it meant. I hold my hand up, like Franco Baresi appealing for offside, to any mistakes you may spot in there.

I also promise you that I have revised and rewritten the pieces from how they first appeared online. Sometimes that is because what I said at the time is no longer relevant, and other times because I simply don't like how I said it. Hopefully that avoids any feeling that you might be buying the literary equivalent of a reheated fish supper.

These are games which wrote key chapters in Italian football history, introduced new stars to the sport or simply sparkled with skill and action. They are, I hope, an antidote to the widely-held view that Italian football is too trapped in tactics and treachery to ever entertain. A round of Serie A matches is, in my view, rarely boring.

An Italian Sunday afternoon, when all the games kicked off at the same time, was something to cherish. You went to the game or tuned in to *Tutto Il Calcio Minuto Per Minuto* and hoped your team would emerge victorious. *Novantesimo Minuto* delivered the scores which saw you throw your *Totocalcio* pools coupon into the bin having missed out on getting 13 results right once again. And Monday morning, across the bar, you argued, joked, insulted and commiserated with other fans. I still miss those days.

So take a little walk with me along a nostalgic stadium tour of the Italian game. The past was not better, it was just different. Some things have improved, others have got worse. What has not changed, however, is the hope in every fan's heart that the game they are about to attend might be an unforgettable one. Those are the chapters of some future book. But, for now, make do with some vintage classics from my own personal archive.

Giancarlo Rinaldi, Dumfries, 2013

Sampdoria v Genoa, November 1990

It is the time when Italian football gets up close and personal. A tight, atmospheric ground with the most British-style supporters in Serie A giving their all. The club names may have changed over the years, but the intensity of the Genoa derby remains undimmed.

The most successful times for the two sides involved in the *Derby Della Lanterna* are both the stuff of history. For Genoa, Italy's oldest club, success was something they savoured most about a century ago. As for Sampdoria, a golden age of the late 1980s and early 1990s is at least a little more fresh in the memory.

But these are still two heavy-hitters of the Italian game. They may have under-achieved in recent times but their colours remain among the most evocative in Serie A. The Grifone in their classic red and blue, the Doriani in those unusual blue tops with a red, white and black stripe across the front.

The tie has been littered with classic clashes since Genoa first played Andrea Doria in 1902. It was not until the creation of Sampdoria in 1946 that the derby acquired its present-day personnel. Prior to that Sampierdarenese and Liguria as well as Andrea Doria tried to knock Genoa Cricket and Football Club off their perch.

In modern times the Rossoblu have often cut the figure of the decadent aristocrat whose fortunes are in decline. Nine Scudetti between 1898 and 1924 have rarely been in danger of being added to. The closest they have come since the Second World War was a fourth place finish in the early 1990s.

Their city rivals have often made the whiff of Genoa's demise more pungent. Born out of the fusion of Sampierdarenese and Andrea Doria in 1946 they were Serie A regulars for most of their early days except for one Serie B season in the 1960s and five years in the Second Division in the late 1970s.

But their Golden Age came between 1984 and 1994 when they won four Coppa Italias, the Cup Winners Cup, a Scudetto, the Italian Supercup and lost the European Cup final.

One of the biggest derbies ever came during that magical spell for the Blucerchiati. In 1990 they were at the peak of their powers under well-loved owner Paolo Mantovani. Genoa were in their second season back in Serie A after five years in Serie B and were brimming with ambition to make up for lost time.

On 25 November that year Samp were sitting top of the table after nine matches with the Rossoblu in midtable. Their attacking partnership of giant Czech Tomas Skuhravy and more diminutive Uruguayan Pato Aguilera had yet to hit its stride. Vujadin Boskov's Doria were favourites for victory in order to keep chasing Juventus, Inter and Milan at bay.

Demand to get into the game was intense. *La Repubblica* estimated that about 20,000 disappointed fans had missed out on tickets for the match – technically a Sampdoria home clash. The two clubs met with the local authorities before the game in order to try to avoid any trouble between two sets of supporters so eagerly anticipating the encounter.

There were fears, however, that the pitch at the Stadio Luigi Ferraris might not be up to such a big match. With heavy rainfall swirling over Liguria, there were question marks over what kind of playing surface might be on offer. It was a chance for both managers to indulge in a little bit of pre-match mind games.

"I prayed it would not rain but it made no difference," lamented Samp's Vujadin Boskov. "I think that gives Genoa a big advantage." But Osvaldo Bagnoli disagreed. "That is another handicap for us," he insisted. "Genoa are a more lightweight side and on a heavy pitch Samp will make their superior strength tell." In the end, however, the weather relented enough to avoid the game being played out in a quagmire.

Two bookings in the opening five minutes set the tone for a passionate affair but it was Genoa who kept their cool to open the scoring 27 minutes in. Aguilera sent Stefano Eranio into the penalty box and he put a lovely curling shot into the top corner of the net out of Gianluca Pagliuca's reach.

Samp stuttered but Bagnoli's side threw them a lifeline early in the second half. Simone Braglia dived at the feet of Roberto Mancini, who appeared to be going nowhere, and brought him down for a penalty. Gianluca Vialli duly converted.

It should have given the boys in red, white and blue the impetus to go on to victory but, after a few chances, it was Genoa who took the initiative. Aguilera had a dipping free-kick saved but thunder-booted Brazilian Claudio Branco showed him how to do it in the 74th minute. The ball was rolled to him before he unleashed a trademark blast which gave Pagliuca no chance.

The Genoani would turn pictures of that goal into Christmas cards to send to their Doriani friends and work colleagues. It gave them an unexpected win and kick-started their season.

"Sampdoria talked a lot about how we were a much poorer side than them," said Branco after the match. "But over 90 minutes I think we were a lot, lot better than they were."

His manager was a little less emphatic. "I wasn't even sure who to play," Bagnoli admitted. "But I took a chance and my numbers came up. I got lucky, who knows how many people before me deserved to win and did not manage?" For a while, at least, it helped cool the fires under his continuing feud with the club's most fanatical Ultras.

Blucerchiati boss Boskov saw his pre-match comments that the derby was a game like any other brought back to haunt him. "It was a game like any other," he insisted. "What was different was that we lost. Now the Genoani can laugh at us. We lost our team play because everyone was trying to be a hero."

The damage was not fatal to Samp, however. They went on to win the only Scudetto in their history having kept a Lothar Matthaus and Jurgen Klinsmann-inspired Inter at bay for much of the campaign. A total of 31 goals from Vialli (who ended as *capocannoniere*) and Mancini helped them finish five points clear of Inter and Milan.

It also proved to be a great year for the Grifone as they built on that triumph. They ended in a memorable fourth place with 15 goals each for Aguilera and Skuhravy. There may never have been a year when the Genoese derby had more to say about the upper reaches of Serie A.

Inter v Juventus, April 1961

Hundreds of people in raincoats or carrying umbrellas huddled round the pitch of the old Stadio Comunale in Turin. They had turned out in numbers too great for the stadium to hold and poured out onto the touchlines instead. Legend has it some of them even ended up sitting in the dugouts that Sunday afternoon in April. They thought they had come to see a title showdown but ended up, inadvertently, provoking one of the most controversial conclusions ever to a Serie A season.

It is tempting to think that the intense rivalry between Juventus and Inter revolves around the Calciopoli scandal of 2006. The vitriolic exchanges from that dark chapter of the Italian game still echo to this day. But the truth is that the Derby D'Italia has been filled with more venom than a killer cobra for as long as most students of the Scudetto can remember. One of its most poisonous plotlines was played out more than half a century ago.

It could hardly be any different between two sides who have played a protagonist's role in both the domestic and European game over the years. Familiarity breeds contempt, just as it has between Barcelona and Real Madrid, Ajax and Feyenoord, Benfica and Porto or Liverpool and Manchester United. In many ways, these inter-city rivalries carry more kick than a lot of clashes between teams from the same town.

In the spring of 1961, Inter and Juve were on collision course for one of their most stunning season showdowns ever. The Bianconeri were reigning champions, inspired by the peerless strike force of Omar Sivori and John Charles. The Nerazzurri were cast in the role of upstarts, hoping to win the Scudetto for the first time since 1954. It ended with a final twist worthy of an Inspector Montalbano novel.

President of the Milanese giants, Angelo Moratti, had gone out and hired Barcelona coach Helenio Herrera to head up his efforts to tear the title away from La Vecchia Signora. Initial results were impressive to say the least as his team thumped home 18 goals and conceded just two in the opening four weeks of the season. Antonio Angelillo – one of the so-called Angels with Dirty Faces from Argentina along with countrymen Sivori and Humberto Maschio – was scoring goals for fun along with South African-

Italian Eddie Firmani and Swede Bengt Lindskog. It looked like Juve had a serious challenge on their hands.

Slowly but surely, however, the rest of Serie A started to get the measure of HH and his troops and began to limit their goals. Nonetheless, they reached the halfway stage of the season at the top of the division and were crowned Winter Champions with three points to spare over city rivals Milan. Juventus were a further point back.

It was at that moment, however, that Carlo Parola's Bianconeri went into overdrive. A run of nine wins in their next 10 matches saw them catch and then overhaul Inter. Suddenly, their clash on 16 April in Turin had the air of a last chance saloon for the visitors. With a gap of four points to bridge, only a win would do.

The events which unfolded that day, the 27th round of a 34-match season, have entered into Italian football folklore. For Interisti, they became evidence of the unhealthy power being wielded by their rivals in the upper echelons of the game. In the eyes of Juventini, sporting justice was delivered when their opponents' attempt to win the Scudetto by "stealth" was ultimately dashed.

The stadium was packed to bursting point and when large numbers of fans forced their way into the ground without tickets they were eventually accommodated around the edge of the pitch. They were within touching distance of the teams, but the match got under way just the same.

"People were just a few yards away," recalled Inter defender Aristide Guarneri. "But I don't think there was any real danger to the players."

However, half an hour in, the referee decided that the game should be abandoned. Juve felt pressure had been exerted by Herrera to secure the decision. Inter felt vindicated when the match was awarded 2-0 in their favour and it was game on for the title once again.

The verdict seemed to breathe new life into the Nerazzurri's Scudetto challenge as they gathered all their resources to draw level with the Bianconeri in the penultimate week of the season. It set up a scintillating final week to the campaign with Juventus due to host a Bari side fighting to avoid relegation while Inter travelled to play a Catania team already safe in midtable.

A play-off for the title looked a real possibility. Until the storm clouds opened with the news that the decision to award the Juventus v Inter match to the visiting team had been overturned. It was now ordered that the game should be replayed. It put the Nerazzurri back to two points behind Juve and with only a slender chance of winning a title they thought was in their grasp.

"We only heard the verdict that sent us slipping back to two points behind Juve when we were already in Catania," said Guarneri. "We went out onto the pitch with our morale at an all-time low and lost 2-0. We felt we had been made fools of."

That defeat handed Juve, who drew with Bari, their 12th title. But the now meaningless match between the two giants of Italian football had still to be replayed. In one of the most bitter fits of pique ever seen in Serie A, Inter sent out their youth team in protest. Among their number was a future club legend, 18-year-old Sandro Mazzola.

"I was supposed to be sitting my accountancy exams that day," he said. "At home they told me I should put my studies before football and I could not go to Turin. I begged and pleaded in vain. But fortunately the headmaster took sympathy on me and let me take the exams in the morning. The club sent a car to the school to take me to Turin and I got there just in time to play the match."

In a strange crossover of legends, Mazzola's first game for Inter would coincide with Giampiero Boniperti's last for Juventus. The future hero of the Nerazzurri marked his debut with a goal – the first of 117 for the club in Serie A – but it was the Bianconero superstar who had the last laugh. Juve rammed nine goals past the hapless teenagers with Sivori helping himself to half a dozen strikes.

"At the beginning we were a bit embarrassed and we didn't want to humiliate them," explained Boni in one interview. "But Sivori was after the Balon D'Or, which he eventually won, and wanted to score as many goals as possible."

Inter would get their revenge the following year with a 4-2 win over Juve in Turin but they would have to wait until 1963 to get the Scudetto. It ushered in a period of enormous success under Herrera with titles gained at home, in Europe and on the world stage. None of them, however, would permanently remove the ill-feeling from a game which scarred relations between the two clubs for generations to come.

"It was an episode which inflamed the passions of both sides," wrote Antonio Ghirelli in his History of Football in Italy. "It put a divide between the two clubs which would become greater over the years due to their mutual intolerance." And it is that distrust, passion and simmering contempt which makes the game one of the unique attractions of Serie A to this day.

Inter v Roma, April 2003

In recent times they have become two of the greatest protagonists of the Italian game. Inter and Roma have crossed swords for major honours on a number of occasions in the last few seasons. But one of their finest encounters came in a season where neither side ended the campaign with any silverware at all.

At the beginning of April 2003, the Nerazzurri found themselves in the familiar position of chasing down Juventus at the top of the Serie A table. Despite hitman Bobo Vieri already having more than 20 goals to his credit, they were three points behind Marcello Lippi's men. Roma, for their part, were cut adrift in midtable – a pretty miserable state of affairs for a side which had been champions of Italy just two years earlier.

Their mediocre league position was not going to stop Roma president, the late Franco Sensi, from stoking up the game before it kicked off. He was at his fine and controversial best, firing from both barrels at any target which came his way. It was vintage stuff.

"We'll come up against Batistuta on Sunday?" he asked reporters before ladling on the sarcasm. "I am so scared, my legs are shaking! Roma pulled a fast one when we sold him. We deliberately tried to put one over on Inter.

"Maybe it won't turn out that way, we shall see," he added. "But I don't feel any affection for him. We paid a lot of money and he had a good first year when he helped us to win the title but the second and third were a disaster. I shouldn't say such things about a professional footballer but he'll only be around another couple of months anyway and then nobody will ever see him again."

Inter legend Alessandro Altobelli was cutting in his response to the Roma chief's proclamations. "If I was Hector Cuper, I'd play Batistuta from the first minute," he declared. "It is dangerous to hurt the pride of certain players, especially great champions like Gabriel. Sensi should have shown a bit more consideration towards one of the best strikers ever to come to Italy and a symbol of Roma's title win two years ago. But, above all, he showed little respect for an important and prestigious club like Inter."

Once the pre-match sparring was over, the two teams got down to business in front of more than 60,000 fans in the San Siro. With Hector Cuper in charge goals were virtually guaranteed at either end of the park when the boys in blue and black took to the field. His team were the league's top scorers at that stage of the season but also boasted the worst defensive record of any side in the top six. Fabio Capello's outfit had even less ability at stopping their opponents from scoring.

It was something of a surprise, then, when their clash reached half time without a goal. It was not for a lack of attacking intent. Inter sent out Massimo Moratti's favourite plaything, Uruguayan ace Alvaro Recoba, to partner Vieri in attack. Ex-Lazio wide man Sergio Conceicao, former Romanisti Gigi Di Biagio and Cristiano Zanetti, and future Newcastle United player Emre Belozoglu were strung across the midfield. Club legends in the making, Javier Zanetti and Ivan Cordoba, were joined by big summer signing Fabio Cannavaro and the eternally injured ex-Milan and Barcelona full-back Francesco Coco at the back. Between the posts was a refugee from Fiorentina's financial collapse, Francesco Toldo.

Roma responded to the Nerazzurri's 4-4-2 with a kind of 3-5-2. Capello's regular travelling companion Christian Panucci, future Interista Walter Samuel and club hero Aldair stood in protection of Ivan Pelizzoli. Flowing-locked Frenchman Vincent Candela and converted forward Marco Delvecchio were on the flanks of grafting midfielder Olivier Dacourt, on loan from Leeds United, and Brazilians Francisco Lima and Emerson. Up front was the magical duo of Francesco Totti and Antonio Cassano.

It would be FantAntonio who eventually broke the deadlock just seconds into the second half. A delicious outside-of-the-boot curler gave Toldo little chance and it looked like Capello's side might be on for a fourth away league win of the season.

Inter, however, wanted to keep their title dreams alive and it would not take long for them to get things back on track. A lovely long through ball from Di Biagio found Vieri who outstripped Aldair to tuck the ball home for his 24th goal of the campaign. Everything was set for a memorable finale.

With about an hour gone, Recoba delivered a typical moment of brilliance to turn the match in the home side's favour. With the precarious balance of a tightrope walker, he tiptoed through the Roma defence before pinging a pinball shot in off Pelizzoli's right hand post. "A masterpiece of class and killer instinct," purred *Guerin Sportivo* magazine at his ninth strike of the campaign.

When Emre extended the Nerazzurri's lead with just 13 minutes remaining it looked like the job was done. Juventus were a goal up in the Turin derby – they would win 2-0 – but at least Inter were hanging onto their black-and-white shirt tails. Or so it appeared.

Capello had already introduced Vinnie Montella for Delvecchio and he then gave his attack a more physical edge by slotting Massimo Marazzina in for Cassano. At the same time, Cuper chose to withdraw the admirable Emre and replace him with the intermittent skills of Domenico Morfeo.

Whatever the reasons, Inter crumbled. Di Biagio bundled the ball over his own goal-line under pressure from a couple of Roma players. Then Morfeo, with one of his first touches, was robbed by Candela who fed Montella and the Little Aeroplane spun a perfect left-foot shot into the bottom corner of the net.

In desperation Cuper sent on Batistuta while Roma shored things up with Damiano Tommasi for Totti. Either side could have clinched a winner in those desperate closing moments. Montella hit a post for the Giallorossi while Batigol, perhaps with the words of Sensi ringing in his ears, also struck the woodwork in the dying seconds.

It would prove to be a near fatal blow to Inter's title aspirations. Javier Zanetti was the first to recognise that fact. "Anyone who wants to win the Scudetto can never relax – they cannot afford themselves that luxury," he said. "That's especially true against a team like Roma who can punish you at the slightest opportunity."

A week later, the Nerazzurri lost the league derby to Milan effectively ending their Scudetto challenge. Indeed, the campaign proved to be a bitter one for both them and Roma. Inter finished second in Serie A and lost out in a famously fiery Champions League semi-final to their city rivals who would beat Juve in the final. The Rossoneri also clipped Roma's wings in the Coppa Italia final. All that was left for fans of a black-and-blue or yellow-and-red persuasion was the meagre consolation of having served up one of the most thrilling matches of the whole Italian season.

Fiorentina v Milan, November 2005

Finding a ticket to an old football match at the bottom of a drawer is like discovering hidden treasure. It flicks a time-travel switch sending the mind scrabbling backwards trying to recall as much detail as possible about the game concerned. It stirs the soul with emotions from another era.

My house is littered with such mementoes, most of which I have been reluctant to consign to the rubbish bin. I hoard programmes, newspaper match reports and countless other ephemera from games I have attended. They serve me well in conjuring up the atmosphere of disappointment, euphoria, rage and delight surrounding many of the fixtures I have witnessed.

Few are more evocative, for me, than a match stub from November 2005 at the Stadio Artemio Franchi. It was Fiorentina's second season back in the top division after the *Inferno* of Serie C2 and *Purgatorio* of Serie B. My father, myself and my best friend decided we were entitled to a little *Paradiso*.

We could hardly have timed our pilgrimage to Tuscany any better. The Viola were on a flying run thanks to the incredible goalscoring feats of Luca Toni. He had 13 Serie A strikes to his name after just 11 matches and the club was sitting in a healthy third place. Their opponents, Milan, were three points ahead in second spot, busily trying to mount a serious challenge to table-topping Juventus. It had all the ingredients for a special day.

We had travelled to Florence by train from Pisa where our hotel receptionist, a Milanista, had taunted us before departure. Imagine, he said, coming all the way from Scotland to see your team lose. Still, he said he hoped we at least got a nice day out. Little could he have guessed what pleasure lay in store.

It seemed that we had no sooner settled in our seats in the *tribuna* – in fact 10 minutes had passed – than Fiorentina were ahead. A Manuel Pasqual free-kick was met, inevitably, by Toni and the home side had the lead. I was definitely stunned at the speed with which the boys in purple had got their noses in front. There was also fear of how powerful the Rossonero reaction might be.

They did not disappoint in that regard, and nor should they have with a side which, looking back, had an enormous technical advantage over the home team. Cesare Prandelli was just starting to mould his side but it had a workmanlike look. Players like Pasqual, Dario Dainelli, Marco Di Loreto, Christian Brocchi, Martin Jorgensen and Marco Donadel were more honest professionals than Serie A superstars. Milan could count on Alessandro Nesta, Paolo Maldini, Andrea Pirlo, Clarence Seedorf, Kaka and Andriy Shevchenko among their number. Heck, they could even afford to leave old Viola hero Rui Costa on the bench.

The visitors started to make their class tell and it was no real surprise when the scores were levelled about 25 minutes in. A great Fiorentina striker of the future – Alberto Gilardino – met a Serginho cross to head home. The usual wringer of emotions had started in earnest.

Push as they might, however, Carlo Ancelotti's men could not make their evident skills tell. The sides went to the interval all square and when they came back out Fiorentina produced another lightning start. In the opening minute of the second period another Pasqual cross fell the way of Jorgensen and he made no mistake to beat Dida. Once again the underdogs had the lead.

Slowly but surely the visitors started to throw everything they had at the home side. Rui Costa came on for Seedorf, Cafu for Jaap Stam and, finally, Pippo Inzaghi for Kaka. The Milanese giants were desperate to get something from the match in order to keep up the pressure on Juve.

They thought they had found their way through about seven minutes from time. A Rui Costa cross was knocked home by Gilardino but the linesman spotted a tug on Di Loreto. It was a fortunate let-off for the Florentines but one which they managed to capitalise upon.

With time ticking away and the supporters' nerve-endings frazzled, it was Toni who settled things. He nodded another goal past Dida with four minutes remaining to decide the game in Fiorentina's favour. The majority of the thousands of fans who streamed out of the ground were delighted.

The atmosphere on the streets was akin to a major trophy victory. Motor scooters buzzed towards the city centre like mad, metallic bees. Car horns hooted along the Viale Dei Mille as if a third Scudetto had been won. Having been playing in tiny grounds across Tuscany just a couple of years previously, the Viola had taken one of the biggest scalps in Italian and European football. In the process they had joined them in second place in Serie A – just five points adrift of Juve. I recall trying as best I could to absorb that special atmosphere.

"A miracle? No, a project," pronounced the Corriere della Sera. "Rather than criticising Milan ... we should recognise this Fiorentina project. We should praise Cesare Prandelli for the astute way he sets up his team. The Della Valles, without spending excessively, have given him a strong side - and he has taken it even higher."

Of course, this would be the season that *Calciopoli* would turn on its head. There were further celebrations in Florence when they thought they had secured a fourth place finish at the end of the campaign to go into the Champions League qualifiers but that was stripped from them with a 30-point penalty. Their spot went to Chievo instead.

A similar fate awaited Milan who received the same points deduction which forced them into the qualifying rounds of Europe's elite competition. Not that it did them much harm, of course, as they went on to win the Champions League in 2007. Juventus, who had finished on top of the table, were relegated and the title was contentiously awarded to Inter.

Still, despite that bitter finale, nothing could quite take away the pleasure provided by that victory over Milan. It seemed like a watershed moment for the Viola who had struggled in their first season back in Serie A but were now clearly building a stronger challenge. Having gone through such turmoil in recent times there was the promise of better days ahead.

Myself, my father and my best friend travelled back to our hotel in Pisa, heads still pulsing to the beat of the car horns on the streets of Florence. We took great delight in taunting our Milan-loving receptionist. Then we settled in for a good meal in the glow of a great victory. I would swear that our red wine that night was among the finest I have ever sampled. And I think I can still taste it, every time I stumble across that match ticket stuck at the bottom of some dusty filing cabinet.

Fiorentina v Juventus, April 1991

Everyone, it seemed, had an opinion. The barista in the town centre cafe, the teacher at the *Liceo Scientifico* and the *carabiniere* at the corner distractedly directing the traffic – they all had something to say on the subject. But none of them seemed able to agree on the final outcome. Would Roberto Baggio really end up at Juventus?

It was the spring of 1990 and Italy was gearing up to host a World Cup but in Florence and its satellite towns and villages they had more parochial matters on their mind. The little lad they had signed up from Vicenza and nursed through knee surgery had rapidly emerged as the brightest talent the nation had to offer. The Pontello family, however, were getting keen to cash in their chips and it had supporters in turmoil.

This was sporting soap opera of the most intense kind. Fiorentina were in the midst of a truly mediocre spell in their history where a relegation dogfight and grim survival seemed to be the order of the day. But in the boy who would become the *Divin Codino*, they had someone to be proud of – an heir to their greatest hero, Giancarlo Antognoni. Unfortunately for them, he was the subject of overtures from their most despised rivals.

The beat of the message from the jungle drums on the Curva Fiesole was growing ever more insistent. Those in charge of the Tuscan club were prepared to do a deal with the "devil" in order to get the best return on their most promising player. And to hell with the consequences.

What gave the potential transfer an even more delicious irony was the fact that the two clubs were on collision course for a UEFA Cup final. Baggio was instrumental in leading the purple troops all the way to that last hurdle. The spoils ultimately went the way of Juventus and, to add insult to injury, the deal to take their finest player to Piedmont was confirmed afterwards. It was as if the sky had fallen in over the Ponte Vecchio.

The rage which had been simmering among supporters for some time spilled out onto the streets. There were uncomfortable afternoons at the club's headquarters as some fans vented their anger in riot and protest. A message had been given out that the days of Antognoni were long gone. This was now a team ready to sell off its prized possessions, rather than do everything in its power to keep hold of them. It was like uprooting the Uffizi for the highest bidder.

If Fiorentina were the prime target for the Ultras anguish, second in line was *La Nazionale*. Gathering at Coverciano outside Florence to prepare their World Cup bid the Azzurri were forced to go behind closed doors. *"Baggio, puttana, l'hai fatto per la grana!"* went the chant of the most irate *tifosi*. "Baggio, you slag, you did it for the money!". It was a crude, bitter and spiteful way to hit out at a player who seemed, in truth, to have been pretty powerless to avoid the record-breaking transfer deal.

If Italy got a hostile reception, worse was to follow when, inevitably, Juventus rolled back into town with Roberto Baggio in their ranks for the first time. The Bianconeri were escorted into Florence by police motorbikes and a helicopter patrolling overhead. It seemed like the city was closer to a war zone than it had ever been before for a visit by the much-maligned *Gobbi* (the Hunchbacks).

It was early April 1991 and the atmosphere for the 28th round of games in a 34-match season was tense. Juventus sat in fourth place in Serie A – not as high as they hoped but still in with a shout of getting at least second spot behind high-flying Sampdoria. Fiorentina, for their part, were fighting to stave off the spectre of relegation.

An air of how much the afternoon meant to the home support was given by the special *Coreografia* thought up for the match. With purple and white card handed out to the inhabitants of the Curva Fiesole, a portrait of the famous Florentine skyline was put on display. It remains one of the most striking scenes ever put on show by a fanbase which is both contrary and inventive in equal measure. If anybody was in any doubt, it was clear that THIS was the game of the season.

This was not the greatest ever Juve side assembled under the guidance of Mr Champagne Football, Gigi Maifredi, but it still looked strong enough to dispose of Fiorentina. Goalkeeper Stefano Tacconi could count on the likes of Nicolo' Napoli, Gianluca Luppi and Brazilian Julio Cesar to shield him from the Viola attack. Little Thomas Hassler ran the midfield along with Giancarlo Marocchi while the attacking options included Baggio, Pierluigi Casiraghi and World Cup hero Toto Schillaci.

The home side responded with more honest endeavour than real class. There was the Brazilian resolve and organisation of Carlos Dunga and the more dubious talents of Czech Lubos Kubik. At the back they boasted decent professionals like Stefano Pioli and Mario Faccenda. Alberto Di Chiara provided some impetus on the flank while the occasionally brilliant Massimo Orlando played the role Baggio had vacated. Up front, Stefano Borgonovo led the line but was now orphaned of a strike partner who had shared nearly 30 Serie A goals with him a couple of seasons earlier.

It was a nervous affair, always likely to be decided by a set-piece. Diego Fuser thumped home a free-kick in trademark style to give the Viola the lead before half time. It was one of eight goals that campaign which left the midfielder as the club's joint top-scorer in Serie A along with Orlando. For his part Baggio had been, in truth, pretty anonymous.

It was early in the second half that he took centre stage, in an unexpected way. Just five minutes in the Bianconeri were awarded a penalty much to the rage of the home support. It was assumed that Baggio would step up to take it with the trademark calm he had shown throughout his career. But things did not go according to script.

Instead, it was Gigi De Agostini who strode forward and missed the spot-kick, provoking howls of derision. To add to the fury of Juve supporters, Baggio was substituted later in the game and left the pitch draped in a Fiorentina scarf. It was a betrayal which some of the Turin faithful could never forgive.

The Viola held on for a nail-biting victory which ultimately helped to ensure Serie A survival. For Juve, the result proved to be part of a downward spiral which would see them conclude the campaign in a miserable seventh place and see Maifredi relieved of his post. Baggio, of course, would go on to score plenty of penalties and help to win honours for the Turin side.

But that afternoon remains etched in Fiorentina folklore. Perhaps Baggio could not turn down the transfer but he could still reject the possibility of harming a club which had done so much for him. It was a rare moment in football when sentiment was allowed to take precedence over all other considerations. The world seemed to stand still as a small gesture said no amount of money could purchase a player's soul. There have been precious few such incidents before or since that day. But, then, there have not been many players like Roberto Baggio.

Inter v Lazio, October 1998

It was supposed to be the "trampoline to the top". League-leading Fiorentina had suffered their first defeat of the season away to Roma, leaving the door open to Gigi Simoni's Inter to move ahead of the pack. The only obstacle on their path was an inconsistent Lazio side which had already drawn three of its four opening fixtures. Surely nothing could go wrong.

But this was not the all-conquering and confident Nerazzurri we have known in more recent times. It was a side which always seemed to be tortured by doubts on the big occasion and, more often than not, slipped up when a chance for Serie A glory presented itself. Once again, like a clown's trousers, it would take only a few moments for the Milanese giants to come undone.

Sinisa Mihajlovic was the instigator in chief for the Biancocelesti in this October 1998 encounter, and his pinpoint set-pieces caused all sorts of problems. It took him about a minute to deliver a first blow to the home side's fragile self-belief. A trademark swerving free-kick was met by El Matador, Marcelo Salas, and Lazio had the lead. It set up an epic encounter.

Inter tried to force their way back into the match with chances falling to Francesco "Checco" Moriero and Ivan Zamorano while, at the other end, Francesco Colonnese did his bit with a crunching tackle on Salas which forced the Chilean to quit the game early. These were signs of a recovery and it eventually came in spectacular style. Zamorano teed up Aron Winter and the ex-Lazio man delivered a thumping shot to put the sides level. He had no reservations about celebrating the goal.

It looked like the home side was getting up a head of steam but the ringmaster Mihajlovic was about to put on another show. First he hit the post with a free-kick, then he forced a corner out of the Inter defence. And then, from the corner, he delivered another pinpoint cross for Portuguese midfielder Sergio Conceicao to nod home and put Lazio back in front.

Inter's brittle resolve seemed to shatter and a long through-ball from Giuseppe Favalli before half-time saw it disintegrate completely. Roberto

Mancini was happy to skip onto the end of the pass and gave his old Sampdoria teammate Gianluca Pagliuca in goal no chance to make it 3-1. Mancio held the ball aloft in flamboyant recognition of his first goal in six months.

"I wasn't worried about it, but I was happy to get it at the San Siro," he insisted afterwards. "Favalli did a great job putting me through, the rest wasn't difficult."

Worse was to follow for Simoni's men as a result of a heated clash which most observers could have forecast from the outset. Diego Simeone and Fernando Couto have never been renowned for their disciplinary records and it was no surprise when they collided. It was Inter's Argentinian who got his marching orders before the interval for stamping on the Portuguese defender.

The man advantage gave Pavel Nedved all the room he needed as he began to lead the Nerazzurri a merry dance in the second half. He skipped clear on the left to deliver a cut-back cross which was dummied by Roberto Baronio to allow Conceicao to grab his second goal of the game. The match was effectively over as a contest.

A last despairing throw of the dice came with the decision to put on young striker Nicola Ventola for Moriero and it threatened to produce some results. However, the final glimmer of hope was extinguished when Nedved met a Baronio cross to make it 5-1. Fans started to filter away from the San Siro with 15 minutes left to play.

They missed, at least, a show of pride through Ventola. He swept home a pass from Youri Djorkaeff in the 77th minute and struck another late in injury time to make the scoreline look a little more respectable. In between times, Nedved picked up a red card to even up the playing personnel but by that stage it made little difference to the final outcome.

"I never dreamed we would score five goals against Inter, we are a great side," beamed Lazio boss Sven Goran Eriksson afterwards. "But football is funny. We score five in a game when we are without Alen Boksic and Christian Vieri and we lose Salas and Mancini to injury. But the team played a great game both in defence and attack. It was our best performance of the season and as well as showing we have great players, we showed we have great character too."

For Massimo Moratti, of course, there were the usual questions about Simoni's position as coach which he tried to laugh off. "Get rid of Simoni? Don't be stupid," he retorted. "Besides, after a defeat is not the right time to make that kind of decision. Quite the contrary, in fact, in defeat I feel closer to whoever is suffering like me. Simoni did not set out to lose the game, it was just an off-night. A very off-night. But it can help us to learn a few things. I am sure we can recover from it, I have faith."

However, the club owner's belief would prove pretty much unfounded. Inter would end the season in a pretty miserable eighth place while it was Lazio who would go on to become credible title contenders. They pushed Milan to the final game of the season but would ultimately miss out on the crown by a single point.

As for Simoni, what had hardly sounded like a ringing endorsement by Moratti proved to be the harbinger of dismissal. He limped on in charge for another few weeks before finally being shown the door. At least he had had the satisfaction of winning the UEFA Cup – also against Lazio – just a few months earlier. But their last league meeting on his watch was a much more painful one. It was also, at the time of writing, the last time the Eagles won a Serie A encounter with Inter in Milan.

Lazio v Fiorentina, March 1995

Italian teams do not generally hand out hammerings to their league rivals. An unwritten law of respect for their fellow professionals means they tend to ease up once they get a few goals clear, rather than humiliate the opposition. The thinking is, at least implicitly, that you never know when you might be on the receiving end of a potential drubbing and hope they will return the favour.

But nobody ever told Zdenek Zeman's Lazio about that arrangement.

The former coach of the famous Foggia side which stunned Serie A has always been something of a taboo-breaker. His swashbuckling approach to the sport produced high-scoring encounters which were against the historic trend of the Italian game. There was always the threat, to quote a Norwegian commentator celebrating victory over England, that they might dish out a "hell of a beating". In March 1995 at the Stadio Olimpico, it was Fiorentina who took just such a pummelling.

Going into the 22nd week of the season the two teams were separated by just a couple of points in the top half of the table. The Viola took a free-scoring reputation to Rome but also a makeshift defence. It would be torn apart by Alen Boksic, Pierluigi Casiraghi and youthful substitute Marco Di Vaio. With the dribbling of Roberto Rambaudi, the drive of Diego Fuser and the skills of former Chelsea boss Roberto Di Matteo and Dutchman Aron Winter they had a top-class midfield at their backs.

Claudio Ranieri took his Tuscan charges to his hometown with attacking in mind. Gabriel Batistuta and Francesco "Boom-Boom" Baiano - a former apostle of Zeman at Foggia - led the line with the sublime Manuel Rui Costa pulling the strings. They should have had more than enough firepower to give young Alessandro Nesta and his defensive colleagues something to think about.

The writing was on the wall for the Florentines within a matter of minutes, however. Casiraghi opened the scoring and the capital club never looked back. Defenders Paolo Negro and former Torino stalwart Roberto Cravero, with a penalty, also struck before half-time. The game was already effectively over as a contest. A penalty save by Luca Marchegiani from

Batistuta before the break ensured there was no lifeline for the team from the Artemio Franchi.

Ranieri tried to rouse his troops by throwing on Firenze born and bred striker Francesco Flachi but there was to be no let up from Lazio in the second half. Future Chelsea forward and Italy Under 21 boss Casiraghi struck early once again and speedy Croatian Boksic made it five before an hour had passed. Only then did the visitors stir as an attacking force with Rui Costa pulling one back and a Batistuta penalty threatening to make the scoreline respectable.

There was to be no such consolation for the boys in purple that day. When Stefano Pioli was sent off for a second bookable offence it opened the floodgates in a one-sided final 10 minutes. Gigi completed his hat-trick, Di Vaio made it seven and Casiraghi, from the penalty spot, completed the rout. It matched Lazio's all-time goalscoring record from 46 years before against Bologna.

"We lost two goals which is a slight blemish," said Zeman, with more than a hint of irony dancing across his lips. "But overall I think we can be satisfied."

Ranieri was more curt with the one correspondent who questioned him. "What would you have done after conceding eight goals?" he asked. "Would you have got angry? That would have been pointless wouldn't it?"

For Casiraghi it was a special game as he seized his chance in the limelight with prolific hitman Beppe Signori on the sidelines. However, he confessed to reporters that he owed his record goal-haul in a single game to a generous colleague.

"Everything goes in spells," he said. "At the moment, everything is going right but I want to thank Cravero for being an altruistic team-mate. He let me take the last penalty because he knew I wanted to get four goals. Until now I had only managed one hat-trick, a long-time ago, for Juventus against Pisa."

The result proved to be the catalyst to a fine end to the season which saw the Laziali catapult themselves up the table into second place behind Juventus. Not surprisingly their 69 goals made them Serie A's top scorers by some distance. Fiorentina slumped into 10th position with the third worst defence in the league.

The final word, however, should probably go to Lazio skipper of the day, Cravero. "A lot of people say it's no fun going to football any more because tactics have destroyed the game," he said. "We showed that is not the case, I think anyone who bought a ticket to see us today can't have much to complain about." The only exception, perhaps, was the travelling Viola support.

Inter v Milan, April 2005

It is one of the most iconic snapshots of the Italian game. Inter's Marco Materazzi leans on the shoulder of Milan's Manuel Rui Costa as the pair of them gaze in disbelief or bemusement at what is unfolding before their eyes. Fireworks rain down upon the pitch of the San Siro in a scene more reminiscent of Dante's Inferno than a Champions League encounter.

It was a night which did little for the reputation of the city or the nation as a whole. That image, or something similar, was flashed around the planet for all to see. The following day, everyone wanted to know if that was typical of Serie A in general and Milanese derbies in particular.

The answer, of course, was no. The two sides do, however, share a mutual and deep dislike. The message en route to the Stadio Giuseppe Meazza is a pretty simple one no matter which team is at home. It flutters on flags and scarves at the stalls which line the way to one of European football's major theatres. "Odio il mio cugino" is the battle cry which splits the city of Milan - I hate my cousin.

The reasons for this familial disrespect are not so hard to comprehend. Both Rossoneri and Nerazzurri have proud domestic, European and international traditions stretching back for decades. Their high-stakes clashes over the years are the kind of encounters liable to breed a little dislike. The fact that they share the same stadium has only made things worse.

Like two surly siblings who simply cannot get along, the success of their rivals has driven each team to greater heights. Milan were the first Italian side to win the European Cup, Inter responded with back-to-back triumphs. The Rossoneri swept all before them under Arrigo Sacchi, the Nerazzurri completed an historic treble under Jose Mourinho. And their Scudetto squabbles are simply too numerous to mention.

Even in this long and bitter history, however, that one clash which brought the Matrix and Rui Costa together in a famous image may well have been the most venomous encounter ever. In the 2004/05 season the UEFA Champions League set the pair on a collision course which saw their trajectories coincide at the quarter-final stage. The stakes have rarely been higher.

The red-and-black half of the divide undoubtedly had the greater reason for confidence going into the two-legged showdown. Their recent European pedigree dwarfed the achievements of the boys in blue-and-black who had to look back more than 35 years for their last triumph. It only served to make their desire to triumph even greater.

Both teams had been impressive on their way to that stage of the tournament. Milan won a group containing Barcelona, Shakhtar Donetsk and Celtic while Inter saw off Werder Bremen, Valencia and Anderlecht. In the last 16, the Nerazzurri defeated Porto and the Rossoneri beat Manchester United home and away to set up their clash in the last eight. That was when all hell broke loose.

Milan won the "home" leg 2-0 thanks to goals from Jaap Stam and, almost inevitably in those days, Andriy Shevchenko. It meant Roberto Mancini's men had their work cut out to turn things around a week later. They tried hard in a game that simmered with nasty tackles, histrionics and temperamental outbursts almost from the outset. But when Sheva struck again on the half hour mark, it looked like the game was over.

To be fair to Inter, they gave a huge effort to try to get back into contention. However, the goal would not come and their frustration grew greater and greater. Hard as it might seem to believe to those who only saw the tail-end of his Rossoneri days, Brazilian goalkeeper Dida was outstanding in thwarting the opposition attack.

Matters eventually became too much for some Interisti to take about 70 minutes into the match. When an Esteban Cambiasso header was ruled out for a pretty soft-looking foul on the goalkeeper, bottles battered down on the Milan goalmouth. Worse was to follow as fireworks started to shower into the penalty area. Almost inevitably, one of them struck Dida.

He was replaced, but the game could not go on. In surreal scenes, Milan half-celebrated their place in the semi-finals but not with anything like the gusto they had enjoyed beating Inter in the last four of the competition a couple of years earlier. The game was awarded 3-0 to the Rossoneri, Inter were fined and banned from their home ground for four games.

"Those were sorry scenes that are hard to understand" said Carlo Ancelotti. "I have never seen anything like it. It is bad for Inter and it is bad for the whole city of Milan. I think it's a question of culture but TV plays its part too. We can't stay here and talk about referees and slow-motion replays all the time."

"The fans' anger after Cambiasso's goal was disallowed was understandable," said Inter's Ivan Cordoba. "But there can be no justification for throwing objects onto the pitch. I am sorry for applauding the ref ironically when he suspended the game, it was an instinctive reaction. But I still don't know how he disallowed that goal, even he couldn't explain it - he said there was a foul on Dida but he couldn't remember who had committed it."

Inter fans got their consolation via Liverpool when the Anfield side came back from three goals down to defeat the Rossoneri in the Champions League final that year. But Milan would bounce back to take the trophy a couple of years later. Only five years on from that terrible quarter-final would Inter finally win a trophy they had dreamed of for so long.

Thankfully, there have been plenty of other Milanese derbies which have produced more edifying action. They stand as examples of some of the finest matches any club should aspire to. But that European clash of some years ago remains one which nobody – not least the clubs involved – would ever want to emulate.

Milan v Napoli, February 1990

They were the deals which helped to write Italian football's narrative during one of its most golden times and they took place less than two years apart. In the summer of 1984, Napoli pulled off the audacious coup of bringing Diego Maradona to the San Paolo from Barcelona. Then, in February 1986, Silvio Berlusconi took ownership of a Milan side going through one of the bleakest periods in its history. From those two acquisitions, an intense and gripping sporting rivalry was born.

Round one went to Diego and his cohorts with a first Scudetto for the Partenopei in 1987. The Rossoneri hit back a year later with a championship win which would build the foundations for European domination. But it was their tussle to take the title belt on the eve of Italia '90 which would truly go down in history.

This was a battle built along the seismic fault lines of Italian society. The north-south divide has long cast up a stereotypical view of those residing above or below Rome (or some other arbitrary point on the map). According to those prejudices, the northerners are a dour and passionless bunch while the southerners are cast as a work-shy group who are happy to live off handouts from the State. It does not make for harmonious relations.

The 1989/90 season saw both football sides at the peak of their powers. It was almost impossible not to be drawn into taking sides. You were either with Berlusconi's European aristocrats, or Diego's South American street-fighters trying to trip them up. Their clashes were unmissable.

For most of the opening exchanges of the 34-match campaign, proceedings went the Neapolitans' way. They were crowned Winter Champions with a two-point lead over Inter, with Milan a further point back in third. They had already convincingly beaten both of their rivals from Lombardy in the San Paolo.

By February, however, the Rossoneri had emerged as the only serious contenders to the Azzurri's crown. In week 24 of the season they were set to clash in the San Siro in a perfect showdown. Victory for Arrigo Sacchi's men would put them on level points with Napoli, defeat would almost certainly decide the title in favour of Albertino Bigon's side.

This was a muddy and miserable-looking Meazza and the visitors appeared uncomfortable from the outset in such grim conditions. Their changed white shirts quickly became spattered in soil churned up from the San Siro surface. On the rare occasions Diego did set sail on a trademark run he found the ball bobbling about at his feet or else was brought crashing down by a scything tackle from his midfield minder Carlo Ancelotti.

Milan sent all three of their Dutchmen, Ruud Gullit, Frank Rijkaard and Marco Van Basten into battle. But Napoli left Brazilian Antonio Careca on the bench nursing a knock and put out only his countryman Alemao to keep Diego company as their Stranieri. The league leaders looked to be happy to play on the break and, initially, they kept the home side at bay.

The first significant chance fell to Van Basten when Giuliano Giuliani parried a shot away which fell into his path. Only a despairing, late lunge by Ciro Ferrara forced the Milan forward to sky his shot over the bar. Napoli were no more than a sporadic force at the other end.

As so often happens in big matches, fate would play a hand in deciding the outcome. In the 35th minute, Roberto Donadoni pulled up with an injury forcing Sacchi to shuffle his deck. On came Alberigo Evani, who would turn out to play a key part in swinging the match in favour of the home side.

The game was scoreless at half-time but early in the second half Evani skipped away on the left flank to deliver a pinpoint cross into the penalty box. A brave dive from Daniele Massaro was enough to break the deadlock. The man dubbed *San Massaro*, Saint Massaro, for his divine knack of scoring important goals had struck again.

"Scoring a goal after half-time calmed everyone's nerves," commented Rossonero legend Gianni Rivera in the stands. "It also underlined that Milan were on top."

Napoli tried to respond by throwing on Careca for present-day Sky Italia pundit Massimo Mauro and a young Gianfranco Zola for an injured Alemao. Their attacking intent, however, was quickly blunted by a goal from an unlikely source. Paolo Maldini rose perfectly to head home a free-kick in the 71st minute – his first Serie A goal in a couple of years.

That strike effectively killed the visitors' resistance and it fell to Van Basten to deliver the coup de grace with the third headed goal of the game, four minutes from full time. Having missed the first seven games of the season through injury it was a phenomenal 15th Serie A strike for the Dutchman in just 17 appearances to that point.

It looked as if the 3-0 triumph had set Milan on their way to the title. They took the outright league lead a couple of weeks later but defeats by Juve and Inter and a drab draw with Bologna allowed Napoli to draw level with just three games remaining. A bitter defeat to Verona at the Stadio Bentegodi in the penultimate round of matches would effectively seal the Rossoneri's fate and leave the door open to a second Neapolitan Scudetto. Marco Baroni duly delivered the goal to defeat Lazio in the final week to clinch that crown.

Consolation would come for Milan, as it so often has, in Europe. Sacchi's side beat Benfica in Vienna to win a fourth European Cup having also triumphed the previous year. It would soften the blow of a title they felt had been "gifted" to Napoli by the decision to award them victory in their away clash with Atalanta when Alemao was struck by a coin from the crowd. In the San Paolo, however, it was one in the eye for their northern rivals and jars of "Berlusconi's tears" were reputedly sold around the city.

The great rivalry began to dissipate soon after as Maradona left and Napoli's star began to fade. When the Partenopei dropped down divisions it looked like it might never be rekindled. But the dawn of the Edinson Cavani age has started hopes that Scudetto tussles can become the club's bread and butter once again, just as they were back in the late 1980s and early 1990s.

Juventus v Milan, February 1982

His parents may have given him the name Giuseppe, but to the world of football he became known as *Nanu* (The Dwarf). A little striker from south of Naples who won honours and plaudits over a playing career spanning nearly two decades. But few games matched up to Giuseppe Galderisi's dismantling of Milan more than a month before his 19th birthday.

The 1981/82 season saw Juventus locked in a bitter Scudetto tussle with Fiorentina. The Viola led the league at the half-way stage but the Bianconeri, reigning Serie A champions, refused to be shaken off. By February the two teams were level on points but the Turin side were running low on attacking options. Paolo Rossi was still serving his ban under the sentences handed out for a betting scandal while veteran Roberto Bettega had suffered serious injury in a European Cup tie with Anderlecht in November and would miss the rest of the season. Giovanni Trapattoni had little choice but to turn to a fresh-faced forward with just three Serie A goals to his credit as Milan rolled into town.

This was not the all-conquering, global-brand Rossoneri we now know, however. They had just returned to the top division after being relegated for their part in the same scandal which had seen Rossi suspended. Silvio Berlusconi's money was still just a dot on the horizon. The side from the San Siro were in the grips of a relegation dogfight with the likes of Como, Cagliari, Genoa and Bologna.

Juve sent out a team which would form the backbone of Italy's World Cup win that summer. Dino Zoff in goals was shielded by uncompromising tough-nuts like Claudio Gentile and Sergio Brio along with the ever-elegant Gaetano Scirea. Antonio Cabrini's marauding runs from full-back would prove highly influential as would the enterprising attacks of Marco Tardelli and Liam Brady's delicate prompting for a front two of Pietro Virdis and Galderisi.

This was a Bianconero side with much of its heart still in southern Italy. Virdis was Sardinian and Galderisi from Salerno. Brio hailed from Lecce and Beppe Furino was Sicilian. Gentile, of course, made them all seem like northerners having been born in Tripoli in Libya. It would earn him the somewhat unfortunate nickname of Gaddafi.

Milan were much more a team in transition. Mauro Tassotti and Franco Baresi were only at the outset of their glorious careers. Also under the orders of future England assistant coach Italo Galbiati were the likes of future World Cup winner Fulvio Collovati, shocking blond midfielder Ruben Buriani and Walter Novellino. On the bench that day was their star Straniero, and best friend of Rino Gattuso, Joe Jordan.

Galderisi started the goal-fest after just 17 minutes with a piece of opportunism that Rossi would have been proud of. His toe-poke beyond Ottorino Piotti caught the visitors' defence napping. His early impact in Turin had been so impressive that Rossi admitted he was worried that he might be sent packing at the end of the season if his young understudy continued to play so well.

However, despite their struggles Milan hit back just before half time. From a poorly cleared Buriani corner, Collovati had strode forward from the back to thump home a piledriver past Zoff. For once it looked like the Rossoneri could trade blows with the big boys again.

The home side were no doubt told at half time that Fiorentina were already a goal to the good in Catanzaro and began to drive forward with renewed vigour. When Cabrini was sent clear on the left he delivered a perfect cross into the middle which was begging to be headed home. Galderisi, standing about five feet eight inches tall, did the honours.

With the Valentine's Day clash slipping away, Galbiati sent on Jordan in the 70th minute to try to ruffle a few feathers in the Juve defence and it produced almost immediate results. A slip-up by Gentile allowed Bob Antonelli – father of current Serie A starlet Luca – to drive home another equaliser. It looked like *La Vecchia Signora* might have been forced to slow her Scudetto-chasing pace.

Galderisi, however, had other ideas. Another galloping run from Cabrini on the left sent a low cross in towards Virdis. His shot was blocked but his strike partner was on hand to fire home the goal seven minutes from time which would finally ensure a Juve victory. It was a bitter defeat for Milan who had finally shown the determination they had been accused of lacking for much of the campaign.

The two points would prove vital to the Bianconeri in one of the most controversial finishes to a Serie A season ever. They won their final game of the season with a Brady penalty in Catanzaro while Fiorentina had a seemingly good goal disallowed as they were held to a 0-0 draw in Cagliari. Trapattoni's men celebrated winning their 20th league title by a single point. Viola fans declared it was "better to be second than to be thieves".

As for Milan, they could not break their downward spiral. They never managed to climb out of the bottom three and ended up being relegated to Serie B for the second time in the space of a couple of years. It would, however, prove to be the making of the club. They emerged a stronger side and gradually rebuilt into one of the powerhouses of European football.

And what of Galderisi? He never quite established himself at Juve and moved on to Verona where he helped them to win their legendary sole Scudetto as top scorer. He would also play for Milan, Lazio, Padova, New England Revolution, Tampa Bay Mutiny and 10 times for his country – most notably at the 1986 World Cup. His managerial career has, so far, seen him work in some of the more humble surroundings of Italian football. But he'll always have the memories of a Sunday afternoon where he played a key role in stitching the second star onto Juve's shirts.

Inter v Cagliari, April 1994

There was a time when even teams who were struggling in Serie A could pretty much guarantee themselves a run in Europe. In no season was this more true than the 1993-94 campaign when two sides who narrowly avoided relegation ended up fighting out a UEFA Cup semi-final. Cagliari would end the Italian season in a miserable 12th position. Their opponents, Inter, ended up one spot behind them.

The Nerazzurri had suffered a grim campaign domestically. Under Osvaldo Bagnoli they failed to get their strike force of young Dutchman Dennis Bergkamp and little Uruguayan Ruben Sosa to gel. It would ultimately cost their coach his job but nonetheless they continued to progress in Europe kicking out sides like Rapid Bucharest, Norwich and Borussia Dortmund along the way.

Standing in their path to a cup final were a Sardinian side also constructed around an imported attacking double act. Julio Dely Valdes from Panama and Belgian-Brazilian Luis Oliveira proved a pretty productive partnership and gave their boss Bruno Giorgi an unexpected UEFA Cup run. Their list of victims included Trabzonspor, Dynamo Bucharest and, in an all-Italian quarter-final, Juventus.

Their first leg in the Sant'Elia proved to be a pulsating tie. Former Genoa man Davide Fontolan looked to have put Inter in the driving seat with an early goal but Lulu Oliveira quickly responded. When Matteo Villa put the ball in his own net on the hour mark it should have been the end of the road for Cagliari's hopes. Instead, they hauled themselves back into contention with an Antonio Criniti strike and an Antonio Paganin own goal. A 3-2 lead to take to the San Siro gave them hope.

"Inter's defeats just keep on coming," read one match report of the day. "We'll go to Milan with our heads held high to try to make the final," said Cagliari President Massimo Cellino, just a couple of years into the job. "It was tough, but I always had faith in this squad." Among the star performers for the home side that night was an ex-Nerazzurro, Gianfranco Matteoli, running the midfield along with the man who would go on to coach Milan, Max Allegri.

While the Rossoblu fans celebrated into the night, all was not sweetness and light at Inter. They had flopped late in the game and the finger of blame was pointed, as it had been for much of the season, at Bergkamp. "I expected more from him, a lot more," said coach Giampiero Marini. "I am very worried, if a UEFA Cup semi-final can't wake him up, I don't know what can." And teammate Fontolan was just as cutting. "I have to thank the people who say I did the work of two," he told reporters. "But if I had to play for two, it means somebody else did not play at all."

It was in these sour spirits that the Nerazzurri took to the pitch of the San Siro to try to book their place in the final. Nearly 60,000 fans turned out on 12 April to see Inter legends like Walter Zenga, Giuseppe Bergomi and Nicola Berti attempt to get the win they needed to qualify. But they got off to a sluggish start, failing to find much inspiration in an opening half hour where hardened professionals like Aldo Firicano and Nicolo' Napoli held firm.

It took a penalty to break the visitors' resolve. In the 37th minute the referee pointed to the spot after a handball from the unfortunate Marco Sanna. It was the slightest of touches, but it gave Inter's heavily-criticised Dutchman a chance to redeem himself. He duly converted to swing the tie in favour of the Milanese side. He completed a fine evening's work by setting up goals for Berti and countryman Wim Jonk to put the game beyond doubt.

"Every so often we show what we are capable of," said Marini after the match. "We've been waiting for a night like that for a while. For the past month we have hardly ever played badly but we've always ended up losing."

"I can't blame my boys for anything," responded his opposite number. "Inter were stronger and played better than us. Up until we went 2-0 down we were in the game but then everything collapsed. For us the UEFA Cup was a dream but eventually things got serious and it got more difficult. We paid for that."

Inter would go on to win their two-legged final with SV Salzburg bringing back fond memories of their European Cup win in Vienna 30 years earlier. Goals from Nick Berti in the first leg and Wim Jonk in the return match were enough to do the business. It was some consolation for a depressing campaign.

The Nerazzurri's victory was part of a triple national assault on Europe's major trophies once again. Parma would miss out on back-to-back victories when they fell to Arsenal in the Cup Winners Cup final. But Milan held Serie A's colours high with a memorable demolition of Barcelona in the European Cup. Cagliari had also played their part in making Italy far and away the most feared country in continental competition. How distant those days sometimes seem now.

Roma v Lazio, March 2002

Francesco Totti might have had a premonition. Or, more likely, he just hoped to have another opportunity to get up the noses of his eternal rivals. When he tucked a T-shirt carrying a celebratory message beneath his Roma top, he may have had an inkling his team was going to produce one of its most special performances to beat Lazio. But even he could hardly have dreamed of his spectacular goal which would crown a crushing win and send him galloping towards Giallorossi supporters to reveal the legend *"6 Unica"* – You Are Unique.

Yet the Rome derby of March 2002 was a game where even *Er Pupone* played second fiddle. The fervent build-up to the match had all been about which striker Fabio Capello would play – Gabriel Batistuta or Vincenzo Montella. Rumours abounded that Batigol was furious when he heard the Little Aeroplane had been cleared for take-off ahead of him.

This was a another colossal clash in the epic annals of the Eternal City, with Roma defending the title they had won the previous year and Lazio still cherishing memories of a Scudetto triumph 12 months prior to that. Nobody needs to raise the stakes in the Stadio Olimpico, but this was clearly a high level conflict. It ended up producing one of the most one-sided matches in its history.

The goals came in a flurry which seemed almost too fast to be believed. Roman derbies are usually tight, intense affairs with the crunching tackles and in-your-face protests to the match officials outnumbering the scoring chances. Not on this occasion. There was an element of disbelief among most observers.

Lazio were forced to send out a makeshift defence and Alberto Zaccheroni decided to go with five at the back to try to better fend off the Giallorossi's attacks. It proved to be a disaster almost from the outset, with even his most tried and tested players looking in disarray. It was the ultimate bad day at the office for Dino Baggio, Alessandro Nesta, Sinisa Mihajlovic, Fernando Couto and Giuseppe Pancaro.

They were sliced open in the 13th minute when a cheeky Totti backheel put Vincent Candela clear on the left and his neat outside-of-the-foot cross was met at the near post by Montella to open the scoring. It was just his second goal of the Serie A season.

Another ridiculous piece of skill by the Roma captain produced the second goal on the half hour mark. He went on a searing run from the half-way line which spread panic through the Lazio defence. When his shot was parried by Angelo Peruzzi, Nesta seemed to stand transfixed instead of clearing the ball and Montella nipped in once again.

Seven minutes later he had his hat-trick. Totti spun in a free-kick from the right wing and he was again the quickest to react to head home. Lazio looked like a team in shock.

They pulled one back early in the second half through Dejan Stankovic and Capello started to look edgy on the Roma bench. He was unhappy that his players had taken their foot off the gas. He need not have worried, Montella had his best goal yet to come.

A thumping left-foot long-range shot found the top corner and the game was beyond doubt. His celebrations were a mix of joy and incredulity that such a perfect night had come his way in the derby. There was only one thing missing, a Totti goal, and that was about to arrive.

The Roma man claimed he had been eyeing up an audacious chip earlier in the match but had been travelling too fast to execute the move. This time the ball came to him perfectly and from outside the box he dinked home a shot that gave Peruzzi no chance. The celebration T-shirt came out and a perfect night for Giallorossi fans was complete.

It was a remarkable game for everyone involved but nobody more so than Montella. Even if he now goes on to become a great coach, he will struggle to eclipse that mild early spring night. Nursing a swollen eye, he admitted to reporters he could hardly believe what had just unfolded.

"On days like this you accept anything – even pain and a clash of heads – because the joy is so great," he said. "It's truly a dream, four goals and back on top of the table, I'll get them to give me the videotape. Stupendous."

Capello was happy to accept his tactics had worked. He could have taken a hammering if Batistuta's omission had cost his side the game. Instead, he looked like a master of his craft.

"I knew Lazio had problems in defence so I went for technique over strength," he explained. "It worked out. Vincenzo is in great form and can turn a match at any moment. "

It was a less memorable night for Lazio coach Alberto Zaccheroni. His plans were blown out of the water in the opening 45 minutes – so much so that he completely revised his tactics and sacrificed Nesta and Dino Baggio for Guerino Gottardi and Karel Poborsky. It worked a little better, but not nearly well enough.

"I feel bitterly disappointed and I apologise to the fans and the club for what we produced out there," he said. "I don't think the problem was the formation we played but the truth is we never got into the game. We were not aggressive enough in midfield and we were too timid in trying to impose our own play."

He was also apologetic for his Italian international defender. "Even the greatest champions have their off-nights," he said. "It was just that kind of game for him."

Nesta, understandably perhaps, preferred to pay credit to the Giallorossi. "We made our mistakes but we were up against a great Roma side," he commented. "They are a team which has found a great set-up and are tough to play against."

It would not quite be enough to deliver another Scudetto. Juventus pipped Roma to the title by a single point but Montella would go on a late season tear, delivering 13 goals which almost brought them glory. As for Lazio, they were a distant sixth, which was enough to take them into the UEFA Cup. And Alessandro Nesta? He packed his bags for Milan in the summer, his last memory of the Rome derby proving to be a particularly bitter one.

Parma v Juventus, May 1992

The summer of 1990 was a memorable one for Italian football. Serie A sides secured a clean sweep of European trophies thanks to Milan, Sampdoria and Juventus and the build-up was well under way for the World Cup on home soil. It seemed the game revolved around the peninsula.

You could have been forgiven, therefore, for missing Parma's promotion from Serie B to make their first appearance in the top flight. They snuck up in 4th place behind Torino, Pisa and Cagliari. Yet their arrival was to prove one of the most momentous in the history of the top division.

Every so often a team comes along and truly upsets the established footballing hierarchy. They take matches which might once have been regarded as foregone conclusions and turn them into epic encounters. And back in the early 1990s, nobody ruffled the feathers of the big boys more than Nevio Scala's side.

Arrigo Sacchi started to get the Emilia Romagna side noticed in the mid 1980s with a couple of seasons in charge which ultimately got him the Milan job. It was not until the gruffly-spoken Scala took over in 1989, however, that the boys from the Tardini made the leap into Serie A. His first season in charge secured promotion - and the Gialloblu never looked back.

It would be hard to overstate the impact the provincial outfit made. They were entering a division which was just about at the peak of its powers with many of the world's top players and a host of European trophies. Yet they hit the ground running and finished their first campaign in sixth spot which allowed them, incredibly, access to the UEFA Cup.

They did it playing some swashbuckling football too. Scala favoured a 5-3-2 formation where the full-backs marauded forward like out-and-out wingers. Long-haired Antonio Benarrivo and converted Fiorentina attacker Alberto Di Chiara, both signed after that first Serie A season, would come to terrorise their fellow defenders across the country.

They quickly became everyone's favourite second-team but they were not content with the role of also rans. A Scudetto would always elude them -

the closest they came was second place under Carlo Ancelotti later in the decade - but they were not long in getting among the silverware. Their first major trophy came after just two seasons in Serie A. And it came against the biggest team of the lot, Juventus.

That Coppa Italia final was the classic clash of the old world order versus the new. Parma were like an upstart little brother to the more worldly-wise Bianconeri. Over the years their fates would become entwined at a lot of key moments. And, in time, Juve would end up plundering the Ennio Tardini for a lot of its stars like Gigi Buffon, Lilian Thuram and Fabio Cannavaro (via Inter). But those days were still a long way in the future.

Scala used the rump of his promotion team from Serie B and started to embellish and enhance it for conflict in the top flight. Goal threat came from hitman Sandro Melli, organisation at the back from the elegant Lorenzo Minotti and midfield geometry from Daniele Zoratto. Among their other stars were a then slimline Tommy Brolin from Sweden and the man they called Il Sindaco (The Mayor) Marco Osio.

Still, they were not expected to trouble a Juve side which had seen off both Milan and Inter en route to the final. When the Bianconeri edged the first leg in Turin by a Roberto Baggio penalty, most people expected them to grab an away goal in Parma a week later which would surely see them home. This was a Giovanni Trapattoni side, after all, playing on the break was second nature.

The Trap used the attacking power of Baggio combined with Toto Schillaci and Gigi Casiraghi to try to get the result he needed in Parma on Thursday, 14 May 1992. An uncompromising back line of Gianluca Luppi, Jurgen Kohler, Massimo Carrera and Gigi De Agostini should have shielded Angelo Peruzzi from much activity. Juve's other Straniero was another German, Stefan Reuter, in one of his last games for the club.

From the outset the Parmigiani set about giving a lie to a league table which would see them finish 10 points and five places behind their opponents. Tough challenges flew in during the opening exchanges but as the game opened up, the home side started to create more opportunities. It took them until late into injury time in the opening period to strike.

Juventini protested at a free-kick given for a foul on Melli but Osio ignored their complaints to swing in a pinpoint ball which the striker headed home past a helpless Peruzzi. The stakes had risen even further.

A Baggio free-kick almost levelled things early in the second period and then Roberto Galia thought he had tied the match only to see it ruled out for offside. Scala's men, however, remained dangerous and about the hour mark they made it tell.

Melli was again the instigator, feeding Stefano Cuoghi who in turn teed up Osio to hit the ball home first time without hesitation. "It was the kind of move that Parma's greater co-ordination had always threatened to provide," I myself reported in my fledgling fanzine *Rigore!*.

Juve played the cards of Paolo Di Canio for Carrera and Antonio Conte for De Agostini but could not turn the tide. Once again Galia came closest to turning the match with another disallowed goal - a matter of millimetres - and Bianconero frustration grew. Their chances finally evaporated when Conte received his marching orders.

As the game ended Parma fans celebrated their first major victory against a side who would become one of their favoured rivals for silverware. Three years later they defeated Juve in the UEFA Cup final while losing the Coppa Italia to them in the same season. In 1997, when Parma had their best shot at the league title, it was *La Vecchia Signora* who denied them. And once again, in 2002, they fought out the domestic cup final with the Emiliani coming out on top.

From almost nothing, Juventus against Parma became one of the classics of the Italian game. But they have gone through tougher times of late. The financial troubles at the Tardini eventually plummeted them into Serie B where the Turin giants ended up briefly in the aftermath of *Calciopoli*.

Nonetheless, it is a tie which retains a certain fascination with its echoes of the times when the two sides stood toe-to-toe for major honours. Juve look the better equipped these days to challenge for major trophies but they can never take victory for granted. After all, their fans can still remember when the Parmigiani were one of their most pesky opponents - both in Italy and on the European stage.

Napoli v Fiorentina, September 1989

It was the goal we all daydreamed of scoring during our school days. With never a thought of passing to a team-mate, you go skipping past opponents on a mazy run before ending it with an ice-cool finish. In 1989 at the Stadio San Paolo in Naples, Roberto Baggio did it for real.

To this day, footage of the strike is the kind to give fans of beautiful football goosebumps. The naive insouciance (why do the French get all these words?) with which the champion from Caldogno dumped defenders on their derrieres is breathtaking. He may not yet have had the ponytail, but he was already well on his way to achieving divine status.

It remains an iconic Serie A goal. The fact that it was achieved against Napoli gave it added symbolism. It was not a change of guard - Maradona had some big games left in him - but it was definitely a kind of coronation. Even Diego saw echoes of his own enormous talent in the way the slender Viola star had sliced open the Azzurri defence.

There would be other great hits from the Codino but perhaps none to match this. There was his deft over-the-shoulder control while in the twilight of his career with Brescia, maybe. Or that one-two with Giuseppe Giannini and hypnotic run against Czechoslovakia at Italia 90. Yet the San Paolo goal is still a signature strike.

There is a freedom and magic about the effort which has the power to transfix the viewer. Baggio seems to do at the highest level what your four-year-old son attempts when kicking a ball across the living room carpet. In a sport often strangled by tactics, cynicism and fear of defeat - this was an act filled with pure childish glee.

When he picks the ball up just inside the Napoli half with space in front of him, it is almost as if a mischievous thought flits through his mind. What if I just ran straight through the best team in Italy? He evades two desperate attempts to hack him to the ground before duping goalkeeper Giuliano Giuliani and finding the net.

The goal was also to be a calling card for the boy the Florentines had signed from Vicenza and nursed through major knee surgery. A bit like THAT goal Alex Del Piero scored for Juve against the Tuscans in a famous

3-2 triumph, it announced his arrival. Fiorentini already knew he was a great player, now the cat was out of the bag to the rest of Italy.

That pushed Baggio through the doorway of being a minor celebrity of Serie A into being one of its elite. It was a role he would never relinquish throughout his time at Juventus, Inter, Milan, Bologna and Brescia. Few players have produced greater reverence or more heated debate.

His strike against Napoli proved to be a futile one, despite also converting a penalty. The Viola were 2-0 up when the home side decided to throw a half-fit Maradona into the match. He fluffed a penalty but gradually the San Paolo side built up a head of steam. Stefano Pioli headed an Alessandro Renica shot into his own net, Antonio Careca struck and Diego set up Giancarlo Corradini to secure the win. The Partenopei ended the season as champions for a second time, the Viola a lowly 12th.

The campaign, however, was a personal triumph for Roby. He finished with 17 goals - one more than Maradona - and his impresario work took his team to the UEFA Cup final. They lost there to Juventus, who rubbed salt in their wounds by signing their prized asset shortly afterwards. It provoked riots in parts of Florence.

Viola followers were left looking back at the amazing strike against Napoli and wondering what might have been. With a little more money and long-sighted owners, could they have made Baggio the heir to Giancarlo Antognoni and built a new era around him? There were indications throughout his career that he gave more of himself when "cherished" at a smaller side, rather than being one of many superstars at one of Italy's big three.

It is all pure conjecture, of course, but it is one of the mysteries wrapped up in a goal that is like unearthing a perfect fossil of the *Divin Codino's* playing progression. It contains all the elements of poise, precision and panache which would mark him out for life. And for that reason alone, Napoli versus Fiorentina will always be a game linked with one of Italian football's finest stars.

Napoli v Inter, February 1980

Even in a city as superstitious as Naples, the omens can sometimes be wrong. The fans turning out for the visit of league leaders Inter in February 1980 had every reason to expect a tense, low-scoring affair. Instead, they were treated to a glorious riot of goals.

These were two old-school Italian sides built on a solid bedrock of rugged defence. The Nerazzurri were a little more expansive but had kept their opponents from scoring in half of their away matches up to that point. Napoli had already played out seven 0-0 draws in their opening 19 games - their goals against total was eight and at home it was just three. The nets at the San Paolo must have been in pristine condition.

Yet it quickly became apparent that neither side had any intention of living up to their defensive reputation. Eugenio Bersellini on the Inter bench and his Napoli counterpart, Brazilian Luis Vinicio, watched their men go into battle in cavalier fashion. It produced the highest scoring match of the entire season for either side.

Bersellini, dubbed Il Mago della Campagna (The Wizard of the Countryside) for his work at provincial outfits like Lecce, Como, Cesena and Sampdoria, had been building his Nerazzurri side for a while. Appointed by President Ivanoe Fraizzoli in 1977, he gradually strengthened his team to take a serious tilt at the title. The subtle left-foot of Evaristo Beccalossi guided his troops, although the inspirational Becca was missing for the trip to Napoli.

Vinicio, for his part, was busy trying to recreate past glories. He had taken Napoli as close as they would get to the Scudetto before the days of Diego Maradona back in 1974-75 in his first spell on the bench for the Partenopei. His return to Naples, after a couple of seasons at Lazio, was more about fighting for survival with a team whose heartbeat was still defensive legend Giuseppe Bruscolotti.

Their week 20 encounter of that 1979/80 season started with a pulsating rhythm. The game swung from end to end before Inter winger Carlo Muraro, in his sixth Serie A season with the club, opened the scoring after 18 minutes. A long, through ball split the Napoli defence and he made no mistake in sliding a low shot past the despairing dive of experienced keeper Luciano Castellini. They could already feel their advantage over city rivals Milan extending at the top of the table.

The home side, spurred on by a crowd of more than 80,000, had other ideas. They had already forced a goal-line clearance from the Inter rearguard and when a free-kick was awarded in the 22nd minute, they took full advantage. A pile-driver shot was deflected off the arm of Inter midfielder Giancarlo Pasinato leaving Ivano Bordon - the eternal second choice to Dino Zoff for Italy - helpless. Pasinato would be substituted moments after his unfortunate part in conceding the equalising goal.

A little after the half hour mark, Inter forged their way back into the lead. It was that man Muraro again who popped up on the back post to head home a lovely right-wing cross by Domenico Caso, signed in the summer from Napoli. Once again the lead would last only a matter of moments.

Hometown boy Giovanni Improta was the hero this time around. He cracked in a right foot shot from the edge of the penalty area which once again seemed to take a deflection before beating Bordon. It was with the scoreline at an already improbable 2-2 that the sides went into the half-time interval.

It would take two of the biggest names in Inter's history to swing the match decisively in their favour. Once again Muraro was involved as in the 57th minute he rose at the back post to nod a cross down for Alessandro Altobelli. The man dubbed *Spillo,* the pin, because of his tall, slim frame, produced a delicious left-foot half-volley from close range to put his team back in front.

Any questions about the outcome appeared to be dispelled about 15 minutes later when the undoubted man of the match Muraro skipped clear on the right. He floated a ball into the box which was met by the onrushing Giuseppe Baresi. He controlled expertly and drove a shot into the roof of the net to make it 4-2.

Yet Napoli refused to go down without a fight. A long-range effort from former Lanerossi Vicenza midfielder Mario Guidetti hit the crossbar but he was not to be denied. With nine minutes remaining, he played a neat one-two on the edge of the box before sliding a shot under the oncoming Bordon to give the home fans hope.

The Azzurri almost pulled off a most improbable comeback draw in the closing stages of the clash. Improta broke clear on the right and, charging in on goal, struck a cross cum shot from an impossible angle. It cannoned off the point where post and crossbar meet to help Inter keep their lead intact and secure another two vital points.

"We risked losing, I seem to remember Napoli were fighting hard down at the bottom of the table," recalled Inter skipper Graziano Bini years later. "And the San Paolo was full as always."

But they held on to win and the victory ensured the Milanese side stayed five points clear of Milan at the top of the table and they never looked like being reeled back in. They clinched the Scudetto with a couple of weeks to spare from Juventus who had overtaken Milan into second place. Napoli would plod on to solid, if unspectacular, Serie A survival with an 11th place finish. In a bitter twist to the end of that campaign, Milan and Lazio would be relegated for their part in the *Totonero* betting scandal.

Despite securing the only Scudetto of his career, Bersellini still seemed a discontented soul. Some commentators wondered if there was anything could make him smile. "We won the title but I'm not entirely satisfied with my team," he said. "I know I am a perfectionist and never happy but too many things which we tried and retried in training did not happen during matches. We might have won the Scudetto this year but I think we played better 12 months ago when our inexperience always ended up costing us dearly."

That was a view echoed, to some extent, by Bini. He said: "I think the year before we were a better team but with the arrival of Caso we filled a gap. Tactically he sped us up - he wasn't fast but he was quick-witted - he was a fundamental part of winning the title."

It was Inter's 12th Scudetto, won by a team which even the club itself describes as *"operaia"* (workmanlike). But for one February afternoon at least they threw off that tag to deliver a most memorable match. It was an encounter which ensured their challenge for the title was a winning one - and left tens of thousands of Neapolitans cursing their luck.

Sampdoria v Juventus, February 1995

Going nearly a decade without a league title is unwelcome for any big side, but for a colossus like Juventus it is almost unthinkable. Yet in the mid-1990s the Bianconeri were stuck in the middle of their longest rut in the post-war era. It would take a player who had already written his name into legend at another Serie A club to help end their drought.

Gianluca Vialli guaranteed himself a place in the Sampdoria Hall of Fame by ensuring they clinched their one and only Scudetto in 1991. He also steered the Blucerchiati to three Italian Cup triumphs, an Italian Supercup and a Cup Winners Cup. From 1984 to 1992 he formed an attacking partnership with Roberto Mancini which brought the Doriani glory beyond their wildest dreams. Everyone expected them to grow old and grey in Liguria together.

But, in Italy at least, you don't say no when *La Vecchia Signora* comes calling. They needed a striker to kick-start their efforts to knock Milan from their position of pre-eminence at the top of the table. A world record fee of about £12.5m sweetened a bitter blow for the Genoese side.

The title did not come overnight, however, despite his switch to Turin's superpower in the summer of 1992. It took until the 1994/95 campaign before it looked as if Marcello Lippi might finally have the mix which could make the Zebras kings of the Italian football jungle once more. But it would need Vialli to shoot down the team where he made his name to keep them on track for the crown.

By the time week 21 of the season came around the Bianconeri were in a strong position with a healthy six point lead over Parma at the top of the league. Their hosts sat midtable but, with an undefeated home record, they were ready to fight tooth and nail in front of the kind of passionate support that only a visit from Juve can create. It was clear that the boys in black and white would need something special to get the victory they craved.

Sampdoria were a side in transition under Sven Eriksson but still carried a host of star names. Along with the strike partner Vialli left behind in Mancini, they also had former Milan greats Ruud Gullit and Alberigo Evani in their ranks, ex-Inter goalie Walter Zenga between the posts, a fresh-faced Sinisa Mihajlovic delivering thumping free-kicks and everybody's favourite baldy winger Attilio Lombardo on the flank. English import David Platt, however, was missing for the late February clash with his old club.

Juve responded with the mix of muscle and magic that had put them on course for their first title since 1986. Angelo Peruzzi was protected by a group of fearsome defenders like Moreno Torricelli, Ciro Ferrara, Massimo Carrera and Jurgen Kohler. The Little Soldier, Angelo Di Livio, patrolled the midfield along with Didier Deschamps and Giancarlo Marocchi. Partnering Vialli up front were the prematurely grey Fabrizio Ravanelli and the positively cherub-like Alex Del Piero.

A quick hug between skippers Mancini and Vialli before kick-off was the only hint of the emotional charge that the match still carried nearly three years after the latter's departure from Samp. That formality made way for a tight first half in which Riccardo Maspero had the best chance for Doria while a trademark Del Piero free-kick was about as close as the Bianconeri got to finding a goal.

The second half, however, was a different story. The home side began to raise the tempo and produced a string of chances. Unfortunately, they all fell to the feet of 'Popeye' Lombardo who clearly had not taken his spinach that morning. He spurned three fine opportunities. Perhaps he had a premonition he would be signing for Juve in a few months' time and did not want to hurt his future employers?

Lippi was smart enough to see the way the game was heading and shored up his side with the pacy Croatian Robert Jarni in place of ADP. It gave his team a greater threat on the break and it was from a fiery counter-attack that they eventually turned the match. Picking up the ball about midway into Samp territory, Vialli shrugged off a despairing Mihajlovic tackle before driving forward to thump a thunderbolt past Zenga at his near post. The Bianconero forward declined to celebrate his first goal against the side where he had made his reputation. With just 10 minutes left to play, it was a blow the Doriani could not recover from.

"A flash of Vialli and the Old Lady is flying," wrote the *Guerin Sportivo*. And on the back of the game it dedicated its front page to a plea to Arrigo Sacchi to call the striker back into the national team. That particular appeal was unsuccessful as Luca never added to his 59th and final cap received against Malta in 1992.

Juve vice-president Roberto Bettega was typically sanguine in his post-match pronouncements. "After a great opening 10 minutes from them, Juve played well and mostly in the opposition half but without creating a lot of chances," he said. "In the second half Samp came out and were dangerous but we got a goal with a great move at a time when we were a bit more hemmed into our own half."

A decidedly grumpy Mihajlovic was less impressed with the final outcome. "We deserved at least a draw," he told reporters. "We played well in the second half and created a lot of chances and hit the post. This must be Juve's year, however, because when they get one shot on target it ends up in the goal."

But he had the good grace to admit he was powerless to stop Vialli's wondergoal. "I was the last man, if I fouled him I could have got sent off," he said. "He is physically stronger than me and I fell. Marco Rossi came across but it was too late. It was a great shot and a great goal - a sign of his power and technique."

In a tragic twist, Juve dedicated the win to Andrea Fortunato who had just rejoined the squad after battling leukaemia. The promising young full-back hoped to don the black-and-white shirt again but it was a dream that he would never realise. He passed away in April before his teammates clinched the Scudetto once again.

Juve never relinquished their lead at the top of the table after the victory over Samp and thus secured the honour they had dreamed about for nine years. They ended up 10 points clear of Lazio and Parma with Milan a further three points adrift. Samp would finish a respectable eighth. Vialli struck 17 league goals, a couple ahead of his teammate Ravanelli. Samp had joint top-scorers that year with Mancini and Gullit finishing with nine strikes a piece.

Vialli's career with the Torinese outfit would have a final cracking epilogue when he helped them to win the Champions League the following year before moving on to Chelsea where he would gather further honours later in his career. Indeed, he enjoyed success at every club he played for having even won promotion with hometown Cremonese at the outset of his career. Few triumphs, however, were more emotional than the day he clipped the wings of a team which had taught him how to fly.

Parma v Milan, November 1995

Do you remember one of the opening scenes from Superman? An ordinary couple in rural America stumble across scorched earth and debris only to discover a gurgling baby inside some kind of capsule. It is an event which will change their lives forever.

Well, for me, Parma versus Milan has been a bit like that for quite some time. In the genteel surroundings of the Stadio Ennio Tardini a footballing phenomenon thumped into the global game in the 1995/96 season. Serie A and the Azzurri have never been quite the same since. It was the game where the world first clapped eyes on Gianluigi Buffon.

And, as Marks and Spencer would say, this was no ordinary debut. This was a debut against quite possibly the strongest side on the planet at that moment. The Rossoneri were at the peak of their powers under Fabio Capello. It seemed like folly to throw in an untested teenager against Roberto Baggio, George Weah, Zvoni Boban and the likes.

Yet he performed as if he had been thwarting the greatest players in the game for years. A first clean sheet of many was his reward and recognition from a wider audience watching on Channel 4 in the UK. The boy was clearly a bit special. Among his finest moments, a sprawling save from Marco Simone and diving without fear at the feet of Weah.

A fresh-faced Buffon told Rai reporters after the game he only found out on the Sunday morning he would play the match. It was something of a surprise as he had expected Nevio Scala to give him his debut against Cremonese earlier in the campaign. It would hardly have been such an illustrious start to his career.

"I thought I was going to play that game and I didn't," said young Gigi in a more thin and high-pitched voice than he boasts now. "Today I didn't think I was going to play and I did. I went out onto the pitch like I was playing with the youth team - maybe that's why I didn't have a bad game, I was calm inside."

"He was Parma's best player," chimed Capello. "We deserved to win and if we did not manage to do so, it was because they had Buffon in goal."

The newspapers of the time had more than a hint he would go on to be something special. "Full marks for the 17-year-old making his debut," wrote the *Corriere Della Sera*. It went on to praise Scala for throwing the teenager into the mix. "The problem of finding a replacement for Luca Bucci has been resolved – permanently," beamed Parma president Giorgio Pedraneschi. How right he was.

The man himself was somewhat stunned by the reaction to his display. Many media outlets claimed he was a nephew of former Milan and Inter great Lorenzo Buffon but his family was quick to point out this was not the case. Meanwhile, young Gigi came to terms with his new profile.

"The phone has never stopped ringing," he said in one interview. "But I am not the kind of person to get big-headed. I'll keep my feet on the ground and try to always give everything I have got out on the pitch. It is nice to receive praise and good marks from the papers but I won't be taken in."

"When I was 12 years old I could have gone to Milan," he told *La Stampa*. "But I chose Parma because it was closer to home. It seemed an easier way to start my professional career.

"But I'm not scared, you can't be if you play football," he added. "During a game you have to respect your opponents but never be afraid of them."

He got high marks for his performance. "Raise your glasses to this 17-year-old goalkeeper who managed to hypnotise Eranio, Baggio, Simone and Weah," purred one review giving him 7.5/10 for his display. "Making your debut against Milan is like a tenor making his first appearance at La Scala. But the boy did it, and how."

It has been onwards and upwards since then, of course. Gigi was a stalwart of a golden age at Parma before making his move to Juventus. There were a few slip-ups in his early days with the Bianconeri but once he conquered some initial nerves he emerged to justify the highest ever pricetag for a netminder.

There has been the odd bum note, most notably over his political views, but on a football front he has been immense. His performances for club and country have made competitors for the goalkeeping gloves wilt and fade away. When he is laid up with injury both Juve and Club Italia feel the loss.

Serie A still regularly throws up a Parma versus Milan clash back in the Emilia Romagna ground where Buffon made his debut in November 1995. They are unlikely to produce a debut which will stand comparison with the one made by Superman. But if they feature a player who goes on to be half as successful, they will already have achieved a lot.

Udinese v Juventus, December 1983

It just might be Serie A's answer to a cold night at the Britannia Stadium. An icy December day at the Stadio Friuli is the kind of test that a pundit might think would be a step too far for a star foreign player, particularly a boy from Brazil. But, back in the 1980s, there was one golden player ready to prove them wrong.

This was a time when the frontiers had not long reopened to *Stranieri* and Italy was plucking the very best of the crop. It is hard not to feel a certain nostalgia, and jealousy, for an era when the footballing world revolved around the peninsula. Nothing signalled this more than Zico's arrival in Udine.

The little Bianconeri have never been the biggest club in the country. Heck, they have rarely been the most significant side in its north eastern corner. But they were still able to lure one of the finest footballers of his generation to come and ply his trade for a brief, magical moment in their history.
Out in the provinces, it is always a special occasion when Juventus come to town. There are plenty of other major sides in the country but nobody quite gets the combative juices flowing like a visit from the big Bianconeri. If you are going to take just one scalp a season, you'd like to be trimming *La Vecchia Signora's* fringe.

When those Turin giants come with Michel Platini in their ranks, the desire to take them down a peg or two is even greater. In the early 1980s, *Le Roi* reigned supreme across European football. What better feeling than to show your skills were a match for one of the finest in the business?

Their clash on 11 December 1983 was a chance to renew a World Cup duel seen in Spain a year earlier. Paolo Rossi lined up for Juve with Zico in the ranks for Udinese. It had been *Pablito* who got the better of the Brazilian in one of the greatest games international football had ever seen. But would the same situation be repeated in their club colours?

The South American star looked puffed up to twice his normal size before kick-off – but that was simply down to the number of layers of clothing he had on. "I have had a cold," he sniffed to touchline reporters. "So I have got to be careful. But once the game starts I'll take all this stuff off."

First blood, however, went to Rossi. With typical penalty box precision he popped up to tap in a cross from the right wing from close range. He wheeled away from goal in a celebration reminiscent of his glory days back at the *Mondiale* in Spain.

But this was not an Udinese side to take defeat lying down. Inspired by the odd touch from Zico, they equalised in a most un-Brazilian manner. Defender Dino Galparoli rose to meet a corner kick and his looping header stunned Luciano Bodini, making a rare appearance in the Juve goal, when it dropped over his head and into the net to level the scores.

Worse was to come for Giovanni Trapattoni's men as a packed Friuli roared its approval for the effort being shown by their favourites. Two ex-Juventini then combined to put the home side ahead. Club legend Franco Causio swung a lovely cross in from the right and it was met by Pietro Virdis to nod the ball home. "I've been threatening to score for a couple of weeks," said the expert striker at half time. "Let's hope it is the first of many."

The visitors had other ideas and their coach decided to shuffle his pack in the second half. Bringing midfielder Beniamino Vignola on for Nicola Caricola proved to be the move that turned the game. He started to take control of Juve's rhythm and gradually gave them the upper hand.

It was from the little Italian's boots that the equaliser was ultimately born. He linked up beautifully with Platini to send a defence-splitting pass into the Frenchman's path. It was not the kind of opportunity he was likely to pass up and he scooped the ball over the goalkeeper into the net to make it 2-2.

That was how the game would finish but not before Zico had done his best to secure victory for his side. First a close range header was easily saved and then a trademark free-kick stretched Bodini to the full. He may not have found the goal in this particular game but the Brazilian tried everything in his power to influence the outcome in his team's favour.

It said much about the quality of Udinese's play that fellow Brazilian Edinho looked disappointed with the final result when he trudged off the pitch. "When we are playing in Udine, we can't settle for a draw," he said.

"But in the first half we were a bit afraid of Juve, maybe a draw is a fair result for both sides."

Platini, for his part, seemed frustrated at how inconsistent his team had been. "When we are ahead we have problems, but when we go behind we play brilliantly," he said. "After we equalised we sat back and we were in trouble. But a point is always something."

It would be enough to build another Scudetto for Juve anyway as they marched on to the title, seeing off Roma by just a couple of points. It was a tougher season for Udinese but they still finished respectably midtable with Zico chipping in an outstanding 19 goals – only to be denied the top scorer's crown by a single goal by Platini. And, on a freezing day in north eastern Italy, they had both proved that star players can always shine – no matter what the weather and location for a match might be.

Fiorentina v Roma, March 1983

It is not the kind of moment a coach draws to his players' attention. So the chances are Carlo Ancelotti has never troubled a team talk with any mention of a goal he scored in front of the Curva Fiesole in Florence many years ago. It was one of his most perfect finishes in an illustrious Roma career before moving to Milan. The only trouble was, it was scored past his own goalkeeper.

The unfortunate header from Il Bimbo (the kid) was the final act of one of the best ever clashes dished up between Fiorentina and Roma. In the glorious sunshine of late March 1983, two of the finest sides the two cities had ever produced took to the pitch under the watchful eye of referee Luigi Agnolin. The Viola had been pipped by Juventus for the Scudetto the season before, while their visitors were already three points clear at the top of the Serie A table with just six games to play.

Yet the match started off badly for the thousands of Romanisti packed into the Curva Ferrovia. The fixture was barely 10 minutes old when Fiorentina's greatest ever impresario, Giancarlo Antognoni, produced yet another virtuoso moment. A sweet, defence-splitting pass sat up begging to be hit by somebody. Young striker Daniele Massaro, who would be canonised by Milan fans for his goalscoring abilities, showed no hesitation to thump the ball home.

"I amazed even myself," he admitted later. "Because my left is not really my good foot. But fortunately I hit it cleanly and with the right swerve and I think it surprised the goalkeeper."

If Roma were unsettled by the strike, they did not show it. Playing with the confidence of a team that knew it was something special, they shrugged off their disadvantage like a minor inconvenience. Within eight minutes the scores were level.

It was another 1982 World Cup winner who was the creator as Bruno Conti showed amazing vision and speed of thought to rip open the home defence. A thumping long pass picked out in-form hitman Roberto Pruzzo and he did the rest. With a defender still to beat, he turned his man with style and sent a low rasping shot past Giovanni Galli. There was still more than 70 minutes to find a winner.

Yet Giancarlo De Sisti's side would not capitulate to a Nils Leidholm team which was clearly on a mission. They traded blow for blow as Paulo Roberto Falcao expertly prompted Roma but Antognoni threatened to send Massaro or Ciccio Graziani through on goal. It was a captivating affair.

It looked to have been decided, like so many Serie A matches, by a referee's decision midway through the second half. A bit of wrestling on the wonderfully named Odoacre Chierico (a Roman born and bred) resulted in the award of a penalty kick which Austrian import Herbert Prohaska duly converted. With second-placed Juventus in the process of throwing away a two-goal lead in a tasty Turin derby, it looked like Roma could just about crack open the title champagne with five games remaining after this one and a five-point advantage in the bag. However, that was when the normally solid Ancelotti intervened.

Fiorentina pressed on the accelerator again and pushed forward in search of a goal which would keep alive their own dreams of European football at the end of the season. Once again it was Antognoni who would prove to be the instigator, although this time in the most bizarre fashion. He scooped a high up-and-under into the penalty area in the hope of finding a friendly Viola head. Instead, it was the Roma midfielder who rose above a pack of players to try to nod the ball to safety. He could only watch helplessly as what should have been a defensive clearance plopped over his own goalkeeper and into the net. It meant that the game was back in the balance and probably the league title too. Suddenly the doubts started to emerge in a team where none of the players was old enough to recall Roma's last successful tilt at the top honour.

There were still 20 minutes to play in Florence but no more goals were forthcoming. Both sides had entertained but ultimately come away with a point less than they had hoped for. Liedholm appeared to be resigned to his side's lack of maturity in a post-match interview. Or perhaps he was simply trying to give his players a verbal boot to the posterior.

"It looks like we are scared of winning," he told a touchline reporter. "We play great when it is all square or even when we are losing. But when we get ahead we seem to leave all that behind and we become insecure, like a small team."

Luckily for *Il Barone* and his calamitous midfielder, it would not prove to be a fatal blow to their title dreams. The Giallorossi kept their focus and managed to grab the Scudetto for only the second time – the first in more than four decades. Fiorentina achieved a more than respectable fifth place but it left them a point short of the last UEFA Cup spot which went to Verona.

And, despite the momentary disaster, Ancelotti went on to have a stellar career. There were numerous honours with Milan and then more managerial triumphs, first in Italy and then in England. Only in the Stadio Artemio Franchi, perhaps, do they still fondly remember him for a rare error which he would probably rather forget.

Lazio v Juventus, December 1994

There was a time, it seemed, when he could never miss. Give the boy an opening from a particular angle on the left hand edge of the penalty area and every shot would trace an inexorable arc to the top right corner of the net. There was little or nothing a goalkeeper could do to stop Alessandro Del Piero as he was starting to carve out his niche in Serie A folklore.

A most difficult artform was made to seem commonplace by Juve's rising star of the 1990s. It almost appeared his physique had been perfectly constructed to deliver just the right amount of swerve and spin to a shot from that position. Slowly but surely most of Italy's defenders discovered to their cost that leaving him even the tiniest amount of space would result in almost certain disaster.

In the 1994/95 season, he was yet to establish himself as being 'da Juve' (worthy of Juventus). He was still considered, by and large, to be Roberto Baggio's deputy at the club. That state of affairs was not to last for much longer.

The Bianconeri were in hot pursuit of pace-setting Parma as the league entered its week 13 round of games. The boys from the Ennio Tardini were on the road to struggling Genoa while Juve set off for a much sterner test in the Stadio Olimpico against a Lazio side which was also on the fringes of the Scudetto hunt. It produced a clash with a better flow than the River Tiber itself.

Juve went into the game missing some of their key players. Gianluca Vialli, Roberto Baggio, Angelo Di Livio and Luca Fusi were all sidelined, effectively taking the spine right out of the team. It was time for some of the new generation to make their mark.

It started out with a controversial moment which could have defined the game. Lazio were convinced they should have had a penalty after three minutes for a foul on Gigi Casiraghi. Even at full time, Zdenek Zeman was still raging.

"If they had given us the penalty we deserved it would have turned the match," he insisted. "For me it was not only a penalty but Angelo Peruzzi should have been sent off. I don't understand why Lazio always finish a match with 10 players and others end up with the full 11."

Despite that contentious decision, Lazio were still able to take the lead after 20 minutes. Peruzzi could only parry away a Beppe Signori cross and wide man Roberto Rambaudi was on hand to thump home the opener. It was little more than their play deserved.

But a moment of foolishness from Roberto Cravero would swing the balance of the game. He picked up a second yellow card for deliberate handball reducing the home side to 10 men before the half hour mark. Even the cavalier Zeman was forced to withdraw Signori to shore up his defence. There was a Bergamo twang to the swear words as an irate little Beppe took off the captain's armband and left the pitch to make way for defender Cristiano Bergodi.

"I understand Signori's outburst," said Zeman later. "Nobody likes to be substituted."

It looked like the striker was right to be infuriated as Lazio started to wilt under Juve pressure. Marcello Lippi took a calculated risk, throwing young forward Corrado Grabbi into the fray in place of Massimo Carrera almost as soon as the home side had gone down to 10 men. It paid off in style.

"I don't think it was brave," said Lippi afterwards. "If you are sure that something is right, then you have to do it. But I am very pleased with the mental approach we showed from the outset. Despite the players we were missing, we always played to win."

It was Del Piero, inevitably, who started the turnaround. In the 37th minute, he strode through the home defence and, despite loud shouts for handball, prodded home an equaliser. Then, early in the second half, it was Luca Marchegiani's turn to offer an involuntary assist as he palmed an Antonio Conte cross out to Giancarlo Marocchi who struck it into the roof of the net to give La Vecchia Signora the lead for the first time.

It was then that Del Piero delivered his finishing masterclass. Seemingly marked by two men on the left wing, he danced between the pair of them before sweeping into the penalty box. He took just long enough to pick out the top corner of the net from an acute angle and swung the match decisively in the visitors' favour.

All appeared to be lost for Lazio when a neat triangle of passes put Corrado Grabbi through to make it 4-1 with less than 10 minutes to play but there was time for a late revival which almost threatened to give them an unlikely share of the spoils. Rambaudi showed admirable persistence to set up Gigi Casiraghi who was happy to narrow the gap against his old team. Then, in injury time, a poor clearance by Alessio Tacchinardi ended up right at the feet of Diego Fuser who made it 4-3. The referee's whistle saved Juve any chance of an embarassing slip-up shortly afterwards.

"We can build towards great success with these players," Juve's Roberto Bettega said as the dust settled on a thrilling game. "The Scudetto is our target, just as it was at the start of the season."

"Doing without two great players like Baggio and Vialli is never easy and that means we were doubly good," added Lippi. "Del Piero is a little champion, now he must become a complete champion, but he has some amazing touches."

"A Baggio-style goal?" said the boy himself. "He remains the greatest, but that was a Del Piero-style goal. We showed that Juve can do without anyone. I need to keep getting better and become a complete player. I am not worried about the future, we are playing on three fronts and there will be room for everyone."

The stirring display spoke volumes about both sides who would emerge as major protagonists in the fight for Serie A that season. Juventus went on to take the Scudetto but Lazio finished an admirable second. With 69 goals at an average of better than two a game, they were far and away the league's top scorers. Their star man Signori ended with 17 strikes, Del Piero with just eight. But there was little doubt, even back than, that yet another major star of Italian football was starting to emerge in a black and white shirt.

Acknowledgements

A big thank you to everyone who made this little book possible. First and foremost my wife Anne for her patience and for believing in me and also my children – Mia and Luca – for sometimes giving me the peace to write it. My parents, too, for putting up with my Italian football obsession when I was growing up. And my cousin, Marco Rinaldi, for helping out with the cover design.

Credit is also due to the Football Italia team for their support – in particular John D Taylor for his help with finding a cover image and also agreeing to provide a foreword. I must also mention Antonio Labbate who was so quick to offer to help publicise these pages.

A debt of gratitude is also owed to the various archives of La Gazzetta dello Sport, Corriere della Sera and La Stampa which I plundered for information as well as countless football fans who have posted videos of vintage games which I have been able to pore over.

Finally, and in no particularly order, the Twitter and internet crew who have followed this project from its first origins to final fruition. Kevin at Serie A Weekly for publishing some of these pieces originally, Adam Digby for being my Juventino amico-nemico, Chris King for helping out with my coffee cup needs and Gino De Blasio for culinary support. And, of course, all the others who have made tweeting a lot more interesting and entertaining along the way. Without that virtual backing, this book would never have got off the ground.

Printed in Great Britain
by Amazon